# Revolutionizing Intimacy

## Navigating Connection in a Disconnected World

Tziporah Kingsbury

Published by Soulful Relating Institute, March, 2018
ISBN: 9781732103306

Editor: Niels Peterson
Typeset: Greg Salisbury
Charts and Graphs in Additional Resources: Love Coach Academy
Bio Photograph: www.camilleportraits.com/
Book Cover Design: Lucinda Rae
    www.prosperitybranding.com/create-your-book-cover/

For further information on The Soulful Relating System, Seminars and Private Mentoring go to: www.soulfulrelatinginstitute.com

DISCLAIMER: While anyone may find the practices, philosophy and disciplines in this book "Revolutionizing Intimacy" to be useful and transformative, it is made available with the understanding that neither the author nor the publisher are presenting specific medical, psychological, emotional, sexual or spiritual advice. Nor is anything in this book intended to be a diagnosis, prescription, or care for any specific kind of medical, psychological, emotional, sexual or spiritual problem.

Wherever there is concern about physical, psychological, emotional, sexual or spiritual issues you are encouraged to consult with a qualified professional. There are many counselors, coaches, therapists, healers who are available and happy to support you.

This book is not intended to offer legal or professional advice. I ask for you to take full responsibility for your choice to participate

To the love and grace that has guided my way. To my teachers and mentors along the journey who have taken me under their wings throughout my life. To those who have danced in the experience of love with me.
To all sentient beings.

May we remember our Humanity, and that we are all in this together, providing safe haven for seed level change. May we be mindful so as to not get stuck on the surface of the water, rather, to dive into the dark deep blue oceans, and address the unseen.

# Testimonials

*"Revolutionizing Intimacy is essential in today's world as a guide to bring us back to deep human connection. What I appreciate about Tziporah is that she LIVES what she teaches and is one of the most honest, authentic and passionate women I have had the pleasure to know. She provides very real, tangible ways to awaken in the body, while offering you the reader her heartfelt guidance in learning new EQ (emotional intelligence) skills to enhance your life and relationships. I highly recommend this book!"*
**Scott Catamas, Emmy Award winning writer/producer and co-founder of the Love Coach Academy**

*"It's about time that we have a book speaking to the importance of Pleasure and Intimacy as our birthright and as a healing force in this world. Tziporah Kingsbury is taking on this subject with grace and expertise. Thank you!"*
**Jaiya, Sexologist & Creator of The ERotic Blueprints™**

*"Tziporah unravels the complexities of intimacy and then warmly and beautifully wraps the reader back up in every aspect of it. Tziporah manages to take the reader on journey reflective of her passion, experience and knowledge in intimacy and interconnectedness. She couples this with daily practices for developing greater awareness, connection and presence, just the prescription for living in love and peace. This book is must read for anyone in a relationship who wishes to deepen their connection not only with a lover, but with themselves as well. To create your special space in this world, look no further than Revolutionizing Intimacy."*
**Maureen McGrath RN Sexual Health Educator, Host of the Sunday Night Sex Show on CKNW Vancouver**

"As we navigate in the world post #metoo with more awareness and discussion on privilege, power, and the unshackling of ourselves from the binds of patriarchy, Revolutionizing Intimacy is the much needed salve for the heart and soul of humanity. With her extensive background in conscious relating, Tziporah effortlessly brings you along a journey of confidently traveling the landscape of your unguarded heart for healing, connection, and divine union. At times, you'll feel as if you have the words of a trusted confidant leading you to necessary yet uncharted territory within oneself. Revolutionizing Intimacy is highly recommended for everyone desiring to truly embody and understand the power of vulnerability as the missing link to inner love, leadership, and mastery."

**Phoenix Muranetz, Sensuality Liberator & Founder of Awakened Woman**

"Tziporah's chapter on conscious uncoupling alone is worth taking a copy of this book home with you tonight. I applaud her fierce heart, keen mind, and gentle, vulnerable way she conveys her story so that readers everywhere can take steps toward living more vibrant, connected, self-expressed lives.

**Reid Mihalko of ReidAboutSex.com"**

*"Revolutionizing Intimacy by Tziporah Kingsbury really is a dynamic and interactive journey of discovery in to yourself and to the deep connections that are possible when you have the tools and the awakened consciousness that come alive and are given so passionately within this gracious book.*

*In a world where we get so lost in the fast paced, action packed imagery, it is a beautiful gift to have an authentic guide to quiet the unconscious noise and help you return to true and embracing connection."*

*Tziporah lays it out for you, calling you to "develop a relationship with the content" so you may continue on this path with a brighter colour and texture of embodiment.*

**Suzanne Rickards Raja, Peak Radiance Mentor at Warrior Sage**

*"Everyone knows that true love starts with self-love. But what does that really mean? Finally, a book that shows us exactly how to stay self-connected. And it's a treasure trove of countless more specific teachings that are desperately needed during these dizzying times. Tziporah's teachings are a breath of fresh air!"*

**Kamala Devi, Co-Author of Sacred Sexual Healing**

*"In a culture that puts little emphasis on knowing one's actual self, Tziporah's contribution with Revolutionizing Intimacy, is one for the ages! In fact, I sincerely believe that if each of us chose to adopt the principles within this book, we would polish off the clunky lead that so often festers between us, revealing a new kind of Golden Age."*

**Robin Sol Lieberman, Author of The Charisma Code**

# Acknowledgments

I did not realize what awaited me on the journey of writing a book. Thinking back to the day a dear friend and publisher said to me, "You likely already have a book written in your decades of writing content, seminars, case studies and mentoring students." It was on this day that I began my journey to expand my passion, to co-create a world where all beings felt safe in their bodies, with their feelings, and to open a new reality in which we remember our humanity again. The journey of putting this living, breathing book into form may have taken only two years, however the content you will read upon the pages has been in creation for two decades. Throughout the writing of this book I have been reminded that it takes a tribe and that we are truly all in this together!

There are many of you near and far, publicly and behind the scenes who have held my hand and heart to uplift the vision of this book and make it into reality. I feel I have been given the greatest of gifts to have so much love and so many solid rocks in my life. From the soul family, to my colleagues and the global family, words can't nearly touch upon the appreciation I have for you.

The brilliant literary architect **Niels Petersen. WOW!!!** Who would have thought the original vision for this book would have turned into what it did. Thank you for saying YES! The day you reflected back to me what you saw in my manuscript was a very exciting day, because you GOT IT! Thank you for all the energy, time, heart and patience you have put forth in this collaboration. To see my writing like a puzzle which we remolded over and over again until it was a masterpiece, was exceptional.

My dearest soul sister **Ashley Rose,** you are such a wise

woman and have always had a way of uplifting me through the edges of my own journey, especially when navigating through my personal relationship transition. Your support made it possible for me to show up clear and to articulate my journey through the page of this book.

This book was selective in where it wanted to be written and certainly choose some beautiful power-spots. **Cheryl Good** and **Seva Khalsa,** you and your home provided one of those unique power-spots that provided me with a safe haven to give birth to the writing process. I am forever grateful for our dyads, fun conversations and for the sanctuary you shared with me.

**Twinkle Marie** a beautiful sweet publisher, soul sister and friend. I am always blown away by the pillars in my life, and you, always so graciously showing up in love and patience, are one of them. Thank you for all you have gifted me by being in my life and the many ways you show up to uplift my life's service into the world.

**Amir Masoud Niroumand** your heart and home provided a haven so many times on this journey. Your kindness in making your home my home inspired me to explore a personal mourning period and to channel it all into this book through the Conscious Relationship Transitioning chapter.

**Tahl Gruer,** you will always be in my heart. What a journey it has been. Thank you for sharing a moment of life with me which birthed many magical experiences throughout our relationship. It was such a gift to have you witness my journey of writing, and to celebrate my path. The grace and presence you showed up with during our conscious relationship transition allowed me to transfer, in real-time, invaluable wisdom onto paper during an emotional period. This, I believe, added a potent chapter of the book on Conscious Transitions. I love you.

Friend and colleague **Scott Catamas**, I appreciate your

skill of facilitation, the wisdom you share in the world and for our friendship. Thank you for sharing the charts and graphics in this book from the Love Coach Academy.

My sweet **Mel Mariposa**, brilliant friend and colleague who has a way with words, thank you for offering me your skills and presence in dialing in the subtitle of this book. I believe the perfect one was discovered.

**The Community at the Abundance Farm**, your home-sweet-home in the solitude of BC provided me the much needed space to complete this book.

A book would not be complete without the masterful artist who created the cover, **Lucinda Rae**. Thank you for your creative genius and patience in all our back and forth during the decision making on the cover.

To my **Parents**, who chose to birth me into this world. Somewhere along the way, you passed on to me that anything was possible. Thank you for loving me and never holding me back, even if you did not always understand my choices. I love you.

To **Lovers, Partners, Relationships** and the Global Tribe near and far, you have been, and continue to be a power-pillar of love in my life. Your reflection is a perfect mirror in my daily remembering of my own untapped wisdom.

To all my **Clients and Students** who have shared so vulnerably. Witnessing your journey and seeing you birth such shining light into the world has been such a gift.

To **all my Relations**, to the trees which so often were my saving grace of peace and solitude, to the earth for allowing me to walk this path upon you, to the sky for providing infinite space to open my heart, to all the elements of nature for the way you make love through me in each changing season. You remind me of my profound relationship with existence itself.

# Table of Contents

# Introduction

I have been exploring the multi-dimensional nature of intimacy and human relating for nearly two decades as a mentor, spiritual guide, writer, trainer and public speaker. When I was young I would question how anyone could put a border on a piece of the earth and claim it as their own. How a world could live in a way where an invisible border instigates fear, separation and war was beyond my ideas of what being alive meant.

In many of my talks, seminars, interviews and private conversations with clients I have witnessed the same thing over and over. My clients experience feeling disconnected. They forget their own feelings, truth and passion, and end up feeling as if they were living for what others expected them to be instead of tapping into the deep intimate reality where they feel safe to really know themselves and live boldly and authentically.

Life and the experiences we have offer us so much wisdom. I do believe our experiences are like love letters from the universe; that to evolve and grow we must open, we must read and feel the words in our body as we read and dive deep into self inquiry. They offer a unique window into the deeper aspects of one's human reality.

This book is about slowing down so you can read those love letters. In it I offer a blueprint to assist you in navigating through your life experiences and to move beyond the right or wrong of them. I am not taking sides in this book. I am offering a wider perspective for humanity to come together again and this begins within your heart and your own actions.

My role as a mentor has always been to create a safe environment inside and out, guided with curiosity and compassion. In such a space you, the explorer, can travel through the vast plains of experience. My intention is to be your guide on the journey and to create the same space in the pages of this book.

# What is Intimacy and Why is it Necessary

I believe that many of the world's issues share a common root, that the people involved lack true connection to each other, and that they fear intimacy. Much of the strife we see happening in the world is due to people being caught up in the struggle to survive, believing they are in it for themselves, alone and misunderstood. They get stuck in a cycle where they have stuffed down the pain and feel gagged, unable to let it out. This situation is just like trying to push hundreds of ping-pong balls under water. The more balls you try to stuff down, the more likely it becomes that they will all burst to the surface, usually in the most inconvenient of moments.

Our fight for survival has turned into an epidemic of "he-said, she-said," of "I am right and you are wrong," when all most of us want is to be heard, seen and understood. Seeing, hearing and understanding each other is the core of sharing intimacy.

I am certain you've had your share of "I'm right" moments. Maybe it was a heated argument, or a disagreement with an employee. You get caught up in fighting to prove a point that you know is right. Or caught up in panic, grabbing at the love you want or the attention you crave. Or you are living in such fear because the people around you have views that are so different from your own that you're stuck pushing everyone else away, and, unwittingly, making the world wrong.

Being taught to fight for what we want, or to fear what we don't understand sets us on a path to war. Not just war with each other, but war within ourselves. All of that competing and striving for significance actually pushes real authentic intimacy aside. While being significant may have value in its own right, this book is about finding harmony so that your existence actually begins to give life, rather than taking it away.

You may think your fight and struggle is really what is going to win you the connection you desire, but I am here to share with you that there is another way. One that is kinder, gentler to your whole being, one that takes into account the ecosystems around us and looks at our lives from more of a holistic place. Here you are actually going to be giving life back to yourself, to increase vitality, passion, peace and health while activating more love and connection, and inspiring the same in others.

Uncaging intimacy is essential in this world where we have become so busy and overstimulated—this world where people have forgotten how to feel, how to be. We hide behind invented images and we act in ways we think others view as appropriate. Sadly, we have forgotten how to allow others deep inside our vulnerable places, inside our real selves.

Yet, how is someone able to allow another into such places, when they themselves are unable to find them, or don't even know they exist? A dive this deep into intimacy with others requires you to become intimate with yourself.

In our past it has been inappropriate for others to see, know about, or even discuss these vulnerable places we all have. This has created a vast separation among us. Deep down inside our souls, most of us yearn to be seen, to really feel, to be understood. Humans desire to love, to feel, and to experience a deep spiritual connection with one another.

How does this need for connection show up in your own life? Maybe you desire more sex, better communication, and love. Perhaps you are working on a project that is going to miss its deadline, and the stress is eating you up. Maybe you have a burning secret that you just need to share with someone. Do you recall a time when you felt one of these needs not being met? On top of this, did your feelings (the mental interpretation of our physiological and psychological changes that happen during a trigger or emotional uproar) get all jumbled up and confusing? Are you unable to very clearly ask for what you want? Maybe you are concerned and thinking, "will I sound weird or needy? Will I offend the other person?" Or, maybe you fear that others may think you are weak and naive. Are you afraid of being too vulnerable? Do you protect yourself by shielding your vulnerabilities, trying to be indestructible? When you feel afraid, confused, or unsafe, do you hold back and keep silent until something just triggers you and all hell breaks loose?

Deepening intimacy is the way to peace. Peace within oneself, peace within a community, within society, and the world. Many of us have been scarred by our imagined stories or conditioned beliefs of what intimacy is. The depth of intimacy I am speaking of is a place where all the walls come down and there can be no hiding from yourself or others. There is no more inauthentic pretending to be someone you are not in order to please another or yourself.

This is a reality where you own and encompass all of yourself, therefore naturally allowing others to see and embrace you in the same light. When you take up this mantle of authenticity, you give one another permission to be you exactly as they are.

This level of intimacy reveals the interconnectedness of our inner world to the world around us, our body, our chi, life-force energy, and all other beings.

As we become less guarded, as we learn to understand one another more, to feel our feelings, to become aware of our chi flow, to feel the flow of nature through and around us—the more our relationship with our body, our being, and others, moves from superficial to deeply rooted. We will move from a place of feeling-wisdom to body-wisdom. This is the place where true intelligence resides.

Intimacy is something to cultivate, to celebrate! When there is more collaboration, more communion, more celebration of each person's unique gifts, we will move from war to peace in everything we do. So many are fighting for this, yet what is needed is a deep surrender into intimate authentic connection with oneself, and then with all beings.

Imagine being in a room with 20 people who disagree. However rather than arguing, these 20 people deeply want to understand each other. There is a quality of curiosity and desire to know why, and how, the others do things, even though there is disagreement. This curiosity and desire to understand open the door to deep connection, and a sense of intimate knowing that would not have been there otherwise. Isn't that a better way?

# Part One

# The Relationship With One's Self

# The Relationship With the One

In my work with clients over the past two decades, I have seen the same questions and desires time and time again. People desire richer intimacy. They desire to be heard, understood, expressed, and to have a stronger sexual connection. My number one way to achieve this is to go deep into silence and stillness.

The inescapable truth at the heart of this book is that all relationships stem from our own center. So the greatest responsibility you have in any relationship is cultivating a rich relationship with yourself—body, mind and spirit. The benefits of creating this kind of relationship with yourself are priceless.

- You exude presence, awareness, and sensitivity.
- You take ownership for all parts of yourself, your emotions, your triggers and reactions.
- You embody and actually become the inter-relating skills we will speak of in this book, and allow them to simply be the means of changing relationships and relating in the world.

Imagine yourself as a gorgeous luxury car that needs tune ups and oil changes from time to time. A well cared for luxury car is an amazing vehicle transporting you and your partner or friends. You are the same. As you develop new practices of self care, cultivating more mindful awareness and self-intimacy, you are keeping your car (your body, mind and spirit) in optimal fitness to be a vehicle for extraordinary relationships.

Vipassana You may be asking, "How is going away from other people and the ones I love going to actually create closer connection?" Well, read on as I share my personal experiences and insights that come from having a dedicated practice of doing just that.

In August of 2015 I began a new experience that would catapult my life, my relationships, my sex and my connection to myself to an entirely new level. I knew it was time for me to go deeper into extended silence and stillness. At home, I had been keeping a regular practice of two hours of self quiet-time after I wakeup each day, a yoga practice and a lot of self-care. While this routine allows me to stay in tune with myself, the full life of being an entrepreneur still has a way of filling me up to the point where I require a deeper break and time away. I'm sure you can relate.

This year I fulfilled that need by participating in a Vipassana retreat. Vipassana is a practice that inspires transformation through self-observation. While in silent retreats often for 10 or more days, one discovers the interconnection between the mind and body. This is experienced when one focuses all their attention on the physical sensations which take place in the body which continually change based on the mind. The intention is to cultivate a balanced mind, compassion and awareness by having no outside distraction and turning inward into observation.

I sit once or twice a year with groups ranging from 60 to 80 participants for such silent retreats. And I have a daily practice when I am at home. Silence and being away from the loud busy world is the biggest gift I can give myself and anyone else in my life. It allows me to return refreshed, centered and in a clear state.

My beloved partner whom I was sharing life with at the time, had many years of Vipassana practice. Being an introvert by nature, I of course loved the idea of not talking or having to talk to anyone for an entire 10 days. That was very exciting for me! Yet even in knowing it was what my heart, body and spirit needed, and with all the stars aligning with such ease and grace to have me at this specific retreat, I still had this uneasy hesitation up until the day before I drove out.

I bet you remember a time or two where your gut and heart were nudging you toward something yet your head got in the way. Those old stories of worry, fear, concerns and what-if's... Can you relate?

My experience at Vipassana was absolutely phenomenal. I have a natural love for deep introspection. But more than that, being as sensitive as I am, I love going inside and feeling my whole being change before my eyes.

My journey was a wild ride; I love riding the edges in life. This 10 day journey was a new up-leveling. There were days I felt manic. One minute, I would feel happiness, the next minute rage and anger. I knew the process: sit, feel, feel some more and witness what happens.

What happened was profound for me. There were sits where I could feel the heat, feel my body temperature changing based on my emotions or thoughts at the moment. I was able to observe a thought and instantly feel how my physiology reacted. I witnessed the open and easy flow of energy turn into contraction and tightness like someone was gripping my whole body (and there was, me)! It was like someone was inside me doing surgery, old injuries coming to the surface in pain, and then disappearing. My bones and joints would pop and crack after every sit, like I was being put back together.

Then it happened. It was as if a shell which was encasing me, one which I had outgrown, suddenly cracked open and fell off. There was a river of energy flowing through my whole body. I felt grounded, clear minded. I was the world and nature in vivid and living colors. There was this:

*I am the joy, the spirit and the vibrancy*
*which thrives at my center.*

This transformative moment returned me to a deeply enriching intimate connection with all of life. This stillness and presence will blow your sexual experiences right off the charts. Yes, it is true. What I keep returning to is that the deeper I go inside, the more intimately engaged I become with the external world around me. All those relationships get juicier, more fulfilling, they become an effortless intimate connection.

Now going inside to get silent and still does not mean falling asleep, checking out or disassociating from the present moment. It means waking up, increasing your awareness of sensation in the body, of thought in the mind and the way the physiological responses occur.

Getting still means you uncover emotions, feelings, the uncomfortable and the pleasurable. You feel it all, watch it, and as you do it will change, transform and change again as only nature can. The entire nervous system, tense muscles, and tissues which hold your old baggage will begin to relax. They relax because you allowed space for the change to happen on its own. You gain more capacity to feel life, to feel touch, to feel breath, to hear other people and to speak your heart in any circumstance. Life really begins to live through you.

You are automatically more sensitive, aware and present. These three qualities are keys to experiencing more intimacy. Life will look brighter because you are less weighed down.

We hold so much contraction in our sexual center, deep within the vaginal wall, the genitals, anus and around the pelvis. When the heart has an emotional upset and unconsciously protects itself, the sexual center closes down. It's that good old fight or flight response. In my experience of Vipassina, those places get cleared, they soften, relax and become more sensitive. That's right. Sexual experience takes on a whole new sensitivity. The quality of connection with your partner increases and getting turned on is easier. You lose the need to orgasm which creates a prolonged ingasm, one where you have free flow of pleasure, of love, of connection. And there is only more to come. Goals disappear entirely from the bodily experience as you shift your perspective from believing you need to surrender into fully feeling the journey to letting the whole body actually live the experience.

As I had mentioned, my journey into stillness has been the focus of my life for nearly two decades. I value and absolutely love experiencing first hand every concept and idea I put out there for you as the reader to experience. Now ten days of silence and sitting for over seven hours a day in meditation during those ten days may not be for everyone. However, any form of stillness can add more to any life.

The bottom line is all the life stories—the emotional baggage, the day to day stressors of work, relationship challenges, unmet needs and limiting beliefs—that create a denser version of ourselves, build up in the tissues and cellular memory. When this happens, we have a tendency to project. That is, we turn our story and emotional upset on another, blaming them for our feelings and upset. It is often easier to point the finger in another direction than to own your part or the core of the emotional trigger.

*Allow Your Feelings To Be Your Guide*

In a world that is so overstimulated, you may not even be aware of your own emotional state, your deep feelings, let alone the sensations you feel in your body from moment to moment. In such a busy life, You may have noticed that you barely have time to taste your food or feel your own breath.

There are goals and deadlines to meet! They control our lives to such a point that even intimacy and sexual connection become goal orientated activities with huge agendas. What happened to feeling the experience?

Has it been lost in the belief it is not safe to feel? Do you sense that you'll never get things done if you stop to feel something? Some of us believe that feelings are scary or bad or not appropriate. They can bring pain, discomfort or pleasure, take your pick.

In 1995 I woke up to feel immense emotional and physical pain. This is when I realized paying attention to my feelings was going to be integral to creating sustainable change. My feelings had an untapped intelligence and it was time to listen. The more one feels, the more one can make empowered choices in life and in relationships both at home and at work.

If I take the time to feel what is happening in my body when, for example, I am reacting to an experience or a thought, I will have the information to describe to someone what's happening for me, and to make a decision based on knowing what I need. Instead, what usually happens is that one does not take the opportunity to feel. Instead they let their reaction play out. They project their own emotional state onto the other person, and begin to blame-shift. This means making the other person wrong and responsible for how you are feeling.

Our modern life is one of constantly seeking tips and goal-orientated ways to get ahead. It so pervades us that we even view intimacy that way: you want to learn how to be a better lover, how to have better sex, how to communicate for success, how to trust more, how to have real, and authentic relationships.

In your pursuit of those goals, you might have experienced all the usual ways to learn through reading, taking classes, going to workshops; yet this only gets information into the mind, but may not truly get you to feel or embody the experiences. The theory is a step, however theory on its own is not sustainable and I don't always consider mechanical action the first step to take.

When someone tries to fix emotional overload and old baggage with mechanical action alone, there is a disconnect at the core level which still remains and the action that started out with all good intentions becomes forced and hard. What's needed alongside the theory, indeed before any action happens, is stillness and feeling. Learning through feeling informs your action because you know more about your own needs.

I am grateful that there are so many professionals like myself whose work is creating a safe space for people to go into the fire, to be there on the journey, with you, guiding you to finally love and understand those parts of yourself that you have been running from all your life. Seek out an expert. It is important because if you don't have a safe space you will simply keep on running. Make this commitment to yourself.

# Your Sacred Space

When you hear the term "sacred space," you may think it has to do with some form of spirituality or religion, but a sacred space is not a specifically religious or spiritual idea. A sacred space is a place where you choose to be present, feel, listen, show up with love and compassion. I like to look at a sacred space as a warm embrace. Somewhere that I know my inner and outer environment is looking out for my highest good.

When a trauma is triggered within the physical and emotional body there is a moment of feeling everything is shaken up, like a train just blasted through your living room. The house is crumbling and the furniture is destroyed. Security seems to disappear. The level of connection, intimacy, trust and feeling one's truth may become scattered. The tendency is to run away from the source of the trauma and find a quiet place to hide. It is essential for optimal healing that one returns to a form of sacred space instead of running away from the situation no matter how scary it may feel.

Creating sacred space is about building a relationship with you and your environment. When we set an intention to have a sacred space we are setting up our internal environment and external environment so we may be present to everything. When we show up to create sacred space it is a field where we are choosing to be more present and available to listen, to feel and to learn from all that presents itself.

If this is a new concept for you, at first this may seem uncomfortable and unnatural. If you have spent your life keeping busy, judging yourself and your choices, overriding your own needs, this may seem out of the ordinary. However today I invite you to take that first step to creating a new you.

## Setting Up Your Sacred Space

Pause, stop and listen and ask yourself what do you and your body need right now. It may be a warm room, a soft bed, a trusted friend who you know will listen. Your sacred space may have candles, incense, blankets and pillows. It may have a warm bath with salts or your favorite essential oils. Your situation is unique to you. For example when I am creating my "room" sacred space, I prefer having no clutter, my ceremonial feathers, sage, candles, my flutes and drum. These obviously won't be with me if I am traveling or in a hotel. The bottom line for my space for meditation or reflection is that it be uncluttered and quiet, and has a few pillows.

So it is possible that all you need to create your sacred space is you and a place to sit comfortably. You make a space into a sacred space simply by having the intention to listen and take the time to love yourself and learn what you need.

When you go to set one up, share with your partner, friends, family or anyone, that you are creating this sacred space. If it is in a room, let your loved ones know this is your special place to go and feel safe and nurtured. Ask everyone to honor that space. It may be that you don't want others in this room or you want to make sure those who enter the room are in a certain emotional state and are centered. You may want no arguing or projecting emotions and feelings in this space.

Set the space. What helps you feel safe and warm and nourished? In this situation when I speak of safe we are talking about what environment will assist you to open up emotionally, be able to go into difficult areas, explore some uncomfortability. Often we require an environment where we are with people who have unconditional love, or a room that has blankets, pillows and is private for us to not be interrupted during our process or journey.

## *The Sacred Space Within You*

Now that you have had time to set up and use your sacred space, I want to tell you about the sacred space which lives right inside of you. It is the place where all other relationships stem from. It is the place where your intimacy, security and truth are born. Sacred space is something that you may cultivate anytime and anywhere.

The truth of the matter is that practice is essential to any kind of development. When you use one of the emotional tools in this book, or do your daily practice, you are not only working on your skills, you are also creating an internal sacred space, one that you carry with you at all times. The more you create the time to do the practice, the more the practice becomes your way of being, and the better you become at accessing that internal sacred space.

This means that you have the ability to create such a self care space for a minute or three minutes during the day whenever you feel the need for a recharge. I invite you to take a three minute breathing break in your office, or presence yourself in an elevator by becoming aware of your feet on the floor, the temperature in the room and what you body is sensing in the moment.

The more present you are, the more aware you are of what you are feeling and needing. You also become more tuned in to your surroundings whether you are on a freeway or in a business meeting or on a first date. This is your mobile sacred space.

# Why Daily Practices

When I was bodybuilding and in the business of educating people in exercise science, the basis for creating lasting change was steadily shifting old habits. We are all capable change. It is simply our old habits that keep interfering. This is why you may have gone to some epic motivational talks, workshops, classes or started diets only to see a few months down the road they fizzle out with old habits sneaking back in, the promised results never lasting.

When I was training people in the gym our time horizon to create a new sustainable habit and shift it into muscle memory was three months. My clients would train with me twice a week. Here they would basically be practicing. They would learn proper body mechanics, alignment, how to breath to create greater presence and ease in what they were doing, and how to execute so as not to injure themselves. These same clients would train twice a week on their own. During this time they would repeat the specific exercises we had practiced together. After three months, the change was more permanent in their body memory. The old habits have had time to be replaced by new habits.

It was the many many repetitions of a small task that created a large lasting change. What is true for the body is true for the mind and spirit too.

Learning happens on various levels. We learn through the mind and the body. For a sustainable change there needs to be practice and routine. The body must feel in order to shift these habits. You may have heard the expression "our issues are in our tissues." Our body truly is where our intelligence lives. Just as an open mind is needed to gather information on how to execute, our bodies are required to feel what it's like to apply the information before we have truly learned.

It is important to set up a conscious daily practice in order to create lasting change, a practice that gets in touch with what you feel. You will vary what you do with your daily practice over time, but some things remain the same no matter what habit you're trying to create. Use the following steps to set up any new daily practice.

**Have a conscious dialog with yourself**— Say out loud that I am choosing to make this commitment for myself to do these practices no matter what! This means, from time to time, you may have to take yourself firmly by the hand and apply some tough love.

**Create leverage to motivate yourself** — What is your why? When we truly feel our why we are able to use this to motivate ourselves during those moments that your mind is saying "NOOOOOO! I don't want to do this," or when you find yourself putting everything else first and your practice disappears. Leverage will help bypass the mind's desire to distract you. More on creating leverage in a moment.

**Create your special space** — This space/room will be dedicated to you and your practices. Note that not all practices will take place inside this room. You will apply many of your practices to daily live experiences as they happen. However this room will be a great place to return to your centered, relaxed place and set your intentions for your day, and to truly ingrain the best habits so they are there when you need to use them. More on creating your special space in a moment.

**Schedule time** — If you find scheduling keeps you committed, do it. If you are a busy person and tend to put others before yourself, scheduling you time would be a good idea. It also simplifies life to just look at your calendar and know that you will be in your self care space for the next five to thirty minutes. Scheduling also assists in calming down your mind.

It is said in many spiritual traditions that in meditation or prayer if you only read or recite the words change isn't going to happen. We must feel and really embody the words for shifts to take place. The body must feel to create change. Feeling gives the body direction.

Motivation is a key to maintaining a lasting practice. It can be hard to create leverage for your own motivation if you've never done it before. You can use this short visualization to help create your leverage point.

1. Close your eyes and bring your attention to the pain, the situation you are in or a specific moment when you were in a heated argument or in an experience that felt bad to you. Imagine that moment and feel what your physiological response is in the body. What is your body feeling? Take mental note.

2. Take a couple of deep diaphragmatic breaths. Add in a couple of sighs and allow your body to relax.

3. Imagine you are now stepping either to the side or forward into a new experience. Imagine your ideal experience, or how you feel after your give yourself self-care, when you felt motivated, clear in flow. Or imagine what that may look like, what you want it to look like. Now really presence yourself to feel what your body is feeling when you imagine the ideal, when you imagine how things could be. Take a mental note.

4. Again, take a couple of deep diaphragmatic breaths. Add in a couple of sighs and allow your body to relax.

5. Open your eyes and ask yourself, which would you rather have, the first scenario (not feeling so good) or the second?

You just created your leverage. You can create new leverage again after you have begun specific practices when you begin to experience the benefits from them. Have your leverage point in your inner filing cabinet for those moments when you feel unmotivated and notice you are beginning to slack on those home practices and self-care.

To create your special space, one of the first things required is building a clear, healthy relationship with your environment. Our environments will either assist us as allies to be present, at peace, feel connected and open, or they will work against us. You can use the sacred space you set up earlier, or you can make a space just for these daily practices.

1. Find a room that will be your designed self-care/ meditative space.

2. Make a sign that says "I am in meditation," or "Please do not disturb, self-care in progress." Choose the words that align with you and your family. You might want to say exactly how long so they know when they can knock again. Clear communication is already starting.

3. Set up the room in a calm and present fashion. You are creating a relationship with your environment. Be mindful that the qualities you desire to have in the room are already present in your actions when you are preparing the space.

4. Make sure you have comfort, back support and head support.

5. Wear comfortable loose clothing.

6. If you use audio recordings, have them all with you and easily accessible.

Creating and honoring uniqueness in our relationships with others begins with a commitment to ourselves. Doing daily practices, keeping our emotional body cleansed, taking care of ourselves in body, mind and soul are ways to honor our own uniqueness. The beauty of a relationship is that we get to learn and grow together.

## *The Manic Mind*

The manic mind keeps you busy, frantic at times, avoiding what a part of you knows would really benefit you. It is a mind that is disconnected from the peace and serenity created by freeing ourselves from the emotional past which lives in our body tissues. The hundreds of thoughts coming in at once, the billions of things that need to get done, those are the workings of the Manic Mind. It is also that moment where your emotional triggers are taking control of your life, there is so much congestion and confusion that you may not know your left from right. You know what I am talking about, I know you do. It may feel impossible to stop. However, you must know your why and feel your why to work with yourself when the Manic Mind creeps in.

You discovered your why during the leverage process which was laid out in the daily practices section previously. Why do you want to change, why do you want to have more intimacy, feel more connected, communicate more clearly, etc? What would that offer to you, your life, your work and your relationships? How would it shift the quality of living for you? This is your why. The why will shift based on the experience at hand and you will come back again and again to this reflection. What is your why?

Your daily practices are all about working your emotional intelligence muscle. They will assist you in self soothing, calming and disengaging. They will help you catch when the Manic Mind begins to take over.

# Breath and You — Gateway to Intimacy

While I was guest speaking one night at a friend's book signing event a woman approached me curious about my work. She started speaking to me about all the areas people did not meet her in her expectations of them. I listened as she spoke a mile a minute which allowed me space to sit, listen and be present. I watched her breath which was strongly contracted from the solar plexus up to her upper chest. Her shoulders were up to her ears and I felt for her body. I started feeling this deep empathy and the desire that her body, her belly, her womb, her sex, all the way down to her feet so wanted to be felt by her. It was like she was functioning without a foundation, like a house with only an upper level and the basement crumbling, stuffed with all the old trash from yesterday with the door tightly locked. I noticed all of this being aware of my own feelings for her which arose as I listened and observed. (Empathy is a radical state of presence wherein you have the ability to only deeply listen and, to the best of your ability, understand what another is sharing or communicating without the need to fix, give advice, or use words or take on their feelings as your own. Empathy is not about taking on another person's reality, it is about loving them exactly as they are.)

Finally she paused and I asked, "What do you need and want?" She looked at me with a puzzled look on her face and said "that's it, I don't know what I want. Everything feels so confusing, I have a hard time stopping and can't feel my belly or take a deep breath!"

One of the things that happens when we have unconsciously suppressed so much—not out of a bad choice, but due to becoming busy, feeling unsafe and an instinct to survive—is that the body contracts and pulls in as a way to hold on to safety. In order to really feel we must have awareness in our lower body, and breath flowing to our lower body and belly. This woman was so contracted, so stuck in the fight or flight or freeze mode, that her mind went into a spin. It affected the fast pace of her talking, keeping her from feeling what she was saying because the basement of her body was so over stuffed it was not accessible.

## *Our Most Intimate Relationship*

Think about this: our breath is the most intimate relationship we will ever have the opportunity to experience. That may challenge you already on your perspectives of what intimacy is. As you move through this book, I invite you to imagine what qualities are alive within intimate moments. A few qualities that come to my mind are presence, awareness, vitality, sensory pleasure, nourishment, feeling alive, sensitivity to everything, openness, vulnerability, joy, a sense that an abundance of life and all of existence is permeating throughout all of me.

The breath is making love to every inch of my body. It is what increases the quality of life by breathing deeper, it keeps us alive simply by its action and without it we would die. It is the first relationship we have upon entering this world and is with us until we transition out of these bodies upon our last breath.

When we open to our breath, it evokes all of these beneficial qualities. It has the power to increase all of those qualities, or block them off from our experience.

Peace begins with communicating with yourself, by being present with your body and emotions. This mean returning to the most intimate relationship you have: the flow of your breath.

The most open you will ever experience the breath is in a newborn. The belly rises and falls effortlessly. They don't push or pull their breath, or control it in any way. When babies are born in optimal health, their breath circulates easily, and this is apparent even to the naked eye.

Over our lifetimes however, we start to want to control what we feel, what we experience. This builds contraction in the physical body and in the respiratory system.

### Controlling the Breath

The breath is always moving inside the body. It flows deep inside the body, penetrating layers most of us aren't able to feel. The breath is loving, unconditionally, whether there is a sense of presence to it or not. There is a very rich intimacy to be had in the relationship to your breath, if you choose to lean in and learn.

This may sound odd to you, but breath is the pathway of communication with our physical and emotional body. It is the communicator with our cells, organs, and body chemistry. It massages the organs, it carries oxygen and nutrients to the cells. The way we feel affects the way we breathe, and the way we breathe affects the way we feel. Think about when you are stressed, tired, scared or in pain. Now think about when you are excited and happy. What was your breathing like during these times? How was it different? Become more aware of your breath in everything you do.

If we block this primary communication pathway of breath, it will have an enormous effect on our actions because it is so interrelated to the intelligence within our physical and emotional body. For example, it impacts our ability to clearly communicate with others. If we are contracted in the body, unclear, feeling anxious, worried or angry, how can we possibly communicate in a way with another in which they will understand us or even want to listen to us? We can't.

Our breath is the one thing we unconsciously control throughout life to control relationships and life itself. We dominate our breath in an attempt to dominate and control our feelings. The number one reason we stop breathing is to try to block out feeling. In fact, the way you control your breath is a good mirror for the way you try to control your relationship patterns.

Controlling your breath can lead you either to limit, or deepen the degree to which you experience intimacy and pleasure, depending on the way you do it. The quality of intimacy in your life is created from the profound relationship you cultivate with your own breath.

Sometimes we get contracted inside the body due to a combination of emotions and a disruptive relationship with the breath. When we are contracted, not breathing easily, and we try to speak, it comes out sounding like we are attacking the listener, even if we don't intend to. Then we are surprised that the other person puts their guard up, resists, and might even run away. Being contracted has, in turn, created interference in your communication with another, causing fear and separation instead of clarity and connection. When we control or stop the in-and-out flow of our breath, we do the same in our relationships.

Recall some minor physical pain, like stubbing a toe. The usual reactions are that you contract your muscles and hold your breath. What happens when you feel scared, sad, upset, worried, angry, etc? Your breath constricts and your reaction increases. When your hold your breath, it become a chronic condition and you hold in all your emotions. In turn, the emotions feel like they are controlling your life. That is because they are! You have succumbed to overwhelm, the stress of fear, and stories that may not even be yours.

The outcome is that your body lives with physical constriction, leading to physical ailments and pain. The old emotions and experiences remain lodged in the cellular memory, like the weeds and rocks stuck in hard soil which has not been tilled for decades. Nothing is able to grow. This leads to very reactive relationships, living today through your past traumas and conditions.

When you choose to take the deep dive and come face to face with these feelings that you have been running from for a lifetime, you have room to share more connection in your world, have more vitality and will experience new levels of intimacy in your experiences. Isn't it worth it?

Now beginning to shift that pattern of emotional constriction can be as easy as learning and shifting your breath pattern. When we open our breath back to circular easeful breathing, the emotions have room to move and shift.

## Awareness of Breath is the Seed for Self Awareness and Transformation

I remember the day my relationship with my breath radically shifted. You may think this happened the day I was born, and that is certainly when the relationship with my breath began, but I didn't truly become aware of my breathing until much later. My first conscious exploration and innately profound relationship with my breath began in the first week of the new millennium.

I didn't see this journey coming. I had spent the previous five years as a competitive bodybuilder, pushing myself to my utmost limits, physically and emotionally. I didn't realize it at the time, but I was actually pushing my body beyond its limits. One day I woke up and found that I could barely walk. I put on about 30 pounds over the next 48 hours! And I knew that the direction my life was taking was coming to an abrupt end.

I hit a new low. Not only was there physiological shock, but I was also thrust into mourning over loss and physical imbalance. I recall about a month of not wanting to leave the home. I was feeling sad, angry, confused and helpless. Even though I started making daily little shifts towards a healthier life, it felt like eternity before I was able to make a big leap.

This new chapter of my journey took me to a small Swiss farming village called Kiental nestled in the peaks of the Alps. This wonderful meeting of breath and body took place in what would become my new home, the International School of Cranial Sacral and Shiatsu. A wonderful group of breathworkers was deep in training to become facilitators of this work, which was new to my experience. They invited me in one day to experience what they called Transformational Breath Work. With my love of adventure and new experiences, I immediately said yes.

They brought me into a huge dojo like room filled with 40 other teachers in training. The room was all natural wood floors and ceiling with an epic view of the Swiss Alps. There was a cushioned mat, pillows and a blanket all ready for me in the center.

They laid me down and began to instruct me on how to breathe. My facilitators invited me to breath in and out through the mouth while they placed their hands on trigger points, a process called body mapping. To be honest it did not matter much to me what they said because I was a hell yes without even needing to know what was going to take place. Have you ever had those moments where something just felt right? This was one of those. I was curious and excited for the unknown and what was potentially going to come next.

Soon they had me breathing in a wave like fashion. I felt immense energy light up in my body, so much that my eyes and mouth contracted shut and my limbs went heavy. I saw and felt for the first time, at an energetic level, the fear and pain within my body directly relating to my health condition. My senses were alive and pulsating with various degrees of emotion from pain, fear and sadness, to joy, exhilaration and clarity. This journey was a profound inner awakening, revealing to me that the breath is a potent transformational medicine that few understand. I knew without a doubt this was a medicine that would impact my personal and professional life like no other. This was something I was to share with the world from that day forward.

When I began understanding my conditioned breathing pattern, I began to understand the fear and the emotional armoring that my body held onto. I saw how that armoring disrupted my physical well being. I became aware of the emotional stories that were attached to these patterns: I have to protect my heart, I have to do it all myself, I can handle it all without any support! It was that good old perfectionist breath pattern.

When I began to cultivate this new relationship with my breath, building an understanding of my conditioned breath pattern, life began to shift for me in profound ways, ways I didn't expect. I found a new source of love for my mother, which gifted me with my nurturing space holding abilities. I began to feel more love, more confidence to speak and share my unique truth, I attracted communities and environments that actually aligned and supported my life and transformational journey.

Becoming aware of my breath sparked enormous and deep change. I ended up staying in Europe for the next six years, nurturing my own inner mother by caring for children as an au pair from Switzerland to Italy, Sicily to London.

I was clearer, more present and saying yes to studying in extraordinary communities, and with some amazing leaders and healers. The contraction around my heart, the control I tried to keep dissolved into truly feeling alive, confident and present. I lost the weight I had gained during my health crisis, and I began to move with greater ease, pain free for the first time in years.

When you awaken the awareness of your senses you are getting to know the most intricate places inside yourself in a most intimate way. To be able to make clear choices and know your needs in the moment takes awareness. It means moving through the years of over-stimulation, numbness, and a robotic nature into more presence. And becoming aware of your senses starts with becoming aware of your breath.

Stoking your self-awareness will begin to build what is called emotional intelligence (EQ). It is the ability to identify and understand your own emotions and to respond to interpersonal relationships with more empathy and compassion. As your emotional intelligence grows, so will your ability to identify and understand your own emotions, feelings and needs; to express compassionately your feelings and needs to another; to exude unwavering presence in listening to another; and to empathize or understand another person's feelings and needs.

When you begin to create more awareness, a sense of curiosity is born. The quality of curiosity leads to change. You become an explorer ready to learn about all parts of the self: your physical body, your reactions, your emotions, your senses, and your thoughts. You are unlearning in order to create a new way of communicating with every cell, body tissue, muscle, bone, feeling and thought in your body and mind.

Getting to know yourself at a somatic level allows you to make quick decisions that are best for you, to know your values and to honor your needs in the moment. It also supports you to be more intimately alive in every circumstance. The Manic Mind is no longer in charge of your intimacy. Now your body can actually feel it.

The way you are breathing today, the specific pattern, the in and out flow, is a conditioned state. You were not born with this breath pattern. It is made up of your life stories and everything you have suppressed along the way to survive. Your breath pattern correlates with your personal issues, echoing the way you relate in your relationships. You know the things that trigger you, the way you react, the way you communicate, the people and experiences you attract to yourself. What you may not know is your breath pattern says it all to an eye that is trained to understand the science of Breathing Analysis. The next important step is to become aware of your own breathing pattern.

## What Does Your Breath Pattern Tell You

Your current breath pattern provides a map of sorts to your unconscious patterning and personality. The way you breathe offers literal and metaphorical information about how you react and respond to your life and relationships. Understanding and revealing the direct tie between your breathing, your life, and your relationship experiences can be incredibly empowering. Understanding your conditioned breath pattern is a key to shifting the way you relate with yourself and others.

It is human nature to control, contract and protect in

situations where there may be danger. Your breath shows all the ways in your life experience where you have unconsciously contracted to feel safe, and the breath and body memory did not fully release or let go of the  tensions due to the way the mind has placed judgment on the past painful experience. Now you live through a filtered lens of the past. We may feel uncomfortable for a moment or for an extended period, and we push this down to survive because life carries on around you. Underneath those tensions, constrictions and breath patterns live all those emotional stories and relational patterns. They are literally living in your tissues.

Experiencing emotional pain is very like experiencing physical pain. Think of a moment when you may have felt physical pain, such as accidentally hitting your leg on a sharp corner, or an emotional pain such as intense grief. The body's initial response is to hold the breath and contract throughout. There is likely be be a scream or an intense expression of words as well. It is the same reaction as emotional pain. The body stays clenched and the breath never fully opens again to what it was prior to the experience. Experiences like this happen continuously in various ways from the moment we are born. Like most humans, you end up so constricted that you're using only about a third of your respiratory system, starved of oxygen and life force, and literally half dead.

A breath pattern is created through these experience. That's why myself or someone who is trained in the field of Integrative Breathwork and Body Mapping has the ability to tell mostly everything about you and your relational patterns by observing your breath pattern.

In the breath patters we are trying to create, the breath intends to flow from a foundation deep into the lower abdomen, through the mid/solar plexus or upper abdomen, and then to the heart and upper chest. This breath will move like a wave building from your lower body, cresting upward. The inhale, which represents the receiving qualities, is the focus. The inhale should be long, effortless, and full (to the degree there is ease), allowing the exhale to be like a quick wave, crashing on the shore without push or force. Think also of a rubber band shooting across a room. There would be no push, it would just fly off quickly, effortlessly. Your diaphragm on the exhale is this rubber band when there is no tendency to control or constrict the breath.

An open efficient breath pattern generally has these qualities:

- The breath moves like a gentle, easeful wave without constriction.
- The breath easily expands down to the lower belly and pubic bone.
- The diaphragm, which rests on the lower part of the rib cage, is engaged. The upper chest is relaxed.
- The breath rises without constrictions through your upper abdomen and chest.
- The exhale is like a crashing wave, quickly and effortlessly releasing to allow the next inhale to come in.
- The breath is connected like a circle, there are no pauses between the in-breath and out-breath.

When you have integrated an open efficient breath pattern into your daily life, your emotional state shifts, patterns clear and your breathing becomes easy. And the primary diaphragm will be in use. The tension in your back and upper chest will be released. In order to shift your breath pattern, you must first become aware of it.

In discovering your breath pattern, the first thing you will need to become aware of is which areas of the respiratory system are being utilized? How much air are you taking in and letting out?

The flow of your breath has several other factors of importance as well:

- Where does your breath go first (belly, chest, lungs…)?
- Where does your breath pause or get blocked?
- How much time is spent inhaling compared to exhaling?

The smallest intricacies of your breath patterns give information on your physical condition, as well as the emotional and behavioral tendencies of each individual person.

## Discovering Your Breath Pattern

The first time I experienced Integrative Breathwork and the profound nature of my breath, my body became heavy, like an elephant was sitting on me. Really! I started to feel and become physically aware of the places in my body where I had created contractions through holding my breath. I felt the array of emotions that were living in those contracted places. It was like a tight fist fighting to hold onto past pains and stories as tightly as I was holding on to my own breath. And this was a turning point for me. I dove into a new world with my breath as my guide, to explore what I had suppressed for so many years. It was time for my personal de-armoring and cultivating a new relationship with my breath—the innate intelligence that gives life.

Start to pay attention to the areas you feel you constrict when you do your daily breath practices, meditation, or even yoga. Your breath gives you information so you can be clear on the actions you need to take. Retraining your breath will shift your quality of life physically and emotionally. It will, also effectively shift your relationships and the level of intimacy and connection you experience.

I would like to say, learning about your conditioned breath patterns does not in any way replace private facilitation or mentoring. However, what it does is empower you to begin to understand yourself and to identify the areas that have held you back, or served you at one point, but may no longer be of service to you now. Learning about your own breath patterns and breath analysis can be the beginning of shifting and up-leveling your life and relationships. Cultivating this new relationship with your breath creates more capacity inside of you to love more, to communicate differently, to trust more, and overall to live more authentically.

*Building a Healthy Partnership with Your Breath*

Retraining your breath pattern will require regular work. You will want to set up part of your daily practice with a focus on breathwork. The following exercise is one of my favorites, its focus is on breathing from the diaphragm. You can use it as part of your daily practice. I also like to use it as a kind of discovery experiment with myself. I would recall times when I would get stuck in certain emotions such as feeling sad or frustrated about something that happened, then I would go through this exercise. I invite you to explore this with yourself too.

Breathing Diaphragmatically:

1.  Sit in a chair with your back supported. Sit in a way that you're able to let your body know it's okay to relax. This is important because your breath, which affects your nervous system, is on guard.

2.  Place your hands on your lower belly under your

navel. Make sure you check in to relax and drop your shoulders away from your ears.

3. Gently open your jaw, now open it even wider. Likely it may be tight and wanting to hold on to that control button.

4. At first allow a gentle breath in through your mouth. Let your exhale take the form of a couple of big quick sighs. You know, where your shoulders let the weight of the world drop off of them?

5. Now begin to silence your out-breath and focus on guiding your breath down to that lowest part of the belly where your hands are gently pressing. See if you are able to push your belly into your hands on the inhale and just sigh out the exhale.

Eventually you will create a wave where the in-breath is like a wave rising and the out-breath is like a wave crashing on the shore.

At first it will likely feel as if you are forcing it, however keep silently saying to yourself "I am relaxed, it's safe to relax and guide the breath to be easy and gentle." At this stage gentleness is more important than volume.

## Breathwork Red Flags

My client Sophie was having such a challenge with relationships. She felt frightened of intimacy and was always endlessly giving until she was empty and felt resentment because she was not receiving the quality of intimacy, care and appreciation she desired.

The first awareness Sophie had in our initial meeting was that she was unable to feel anything in her body from the solar plexus down and unable to breath any deeper than her chest.

If you recall, it is the same set of conditions as the woman who approached me at the book signing. It is an unfortunately common breathing pattern.

This pattern is defined by the breath beginning in a contracted solar plexus on the inhale, and the exhale is held back, hard to let go of. This blocks the flow of breath into the lower abdominal area and restricts the full use of the primary diaphragmatic muscle. It also keeps the pressure building upward, as the breath is also constricted in the chest. This pattern is often the response to controlling behavior, perfectionism, and it shows up in people who feel they have to get things right and they don't feel supported.

Be compassionate with yourself. It takes time, patience and attention to shift old habits like a conditioned breathing pattern. Outside of your daily practice, you can check in with yourself during the day to make sure you haven't slipped back into a constricted, tight, limited breathing pattern. Look for these red flags as a sign that you've slipped back into a bad pattern:

- Breathing only in the upper chest.
- Controlling and holding onto the exhale.
- Extreme tension in the solar plexus where the breath is unable to reach down to the belly.
- You have breath in you lower respiratory system but the chest is constricted and difficult to breathe into.

Checking in regularly with your breathing will really set the habit of awareness of your breath. And awareness of yourself is the big goal here. It all starts with breath.

# Cultivating Awareness

The traumatic ups and downs of life leave behind layers of protection which reside in the emotional and energy bodies. For some, those layers of protection manifest in the physical body as well. Those old emotional scars find creative ways to disassociate someone from sensing, from feeling joy, and even pleasure. They keep one disconnected or in unhealthy relationships.

Our connection to our own selves all starts with our connection to our environment. This issue lies at the heart of so many of the issues of the day in that most of the world is disconnected from their respective environments. It is taught in societies the world over that achievement is all that matters. Achieve a high ranking business, earn A's on your report cards, win the spelling bee, get first place in an athletic race, become the prom king or queen. Often it is taught that these achievements are far more important than the experiences which lead up to them. Children develop an emotional importance on what it means to attain these things and if they achieve anything less it is the end of the world. For some it has been. Feeling worthless, feeling unloved, feeling unattractive leads to settling.

Remember the ice skating drama with Nancy Kerrigan and Tonya Harding? Harding had Kerrigan attacked in an attempt to keep her from competing. It was violent and was all based on the importance of achieving a goal no matter who was hurt in the process. I can imagine the pressure put on athletes in competition that potentially adds to this conflict of winning over caring. The emphasis on achievement in the skating world at the time left these athletes so disconnected from each other that one ended up attacking her own Olympic team mate. Cultivating awareness begins to break that disconnection down.

The more aware we are the more it impacts us in making

different choices. Awareness means we feel more, we are sensitive to life, to others, to our inner state. From this place we actually make empowered choices that serve the whole. We started our journey with awareness by focusing on the breath. Now, we will extend that awareness to encompass our entire physical and emotional bodies.

We are alive, yes I am here to remind you that you are alive! Imagine that. Have you stopped long enough today to hear the sounds of the birds, smell the roses, smile at the people you are walking past on the street? Have you shared with a colleague what you appreciate about them just because? These are the moments where you connect to the things around you, to your environment, they are the pathway to more self-awareness.

When you move with this sense of presence and awareness more of you will continue to become available. You will feel more life, more vitality, more joy, more creativity and this will only attract more of the same to you, from the bedroom to the boardroom.

The five years of my life I spent as a competitive bodybuilder came prior to my life of yoga, mindfulness and breathwork. It was a very disciplined, less aware way to live for me at the time. As a bodybuilder I set goals, was extremely disciplined and trained myself to always push beyond my own limits, which sometimes meant not fully listening to my whole body. I lived by the old statement "no pain, no gain." It is what made me so good at what I did.

I was smart in the sense that proper form was important to me when working with weights and resistance. It's tempting to break form to try to squeeze in that one last rep, but breaking form while weight training is how many athletes end up injuring themselves. I figured that if I kept form, I could safely push past the pain and ignore what my body was telling me it needed. Think about all the ways you push past your pain point in your life. Eventually my competitive goals became my only focus: to reach a certain level of conditioning and lose a certain percentage of body fat per day until I got up on stage for the competition. When my body began to speak really loudly to me in the months prior to collapsing, I saw that there were signals if I had only been present enough to hear them.

Our bodies hold an intelligence, as do our emotional bodies. That intelligence always communicates to us through feeling. Many have lost touch with that relationship with their feelings and the sensations in their body, or may have yet to experience it. If I had listened and stopped sooner, my body may have not had to reacted so extremely in order to get my attention.

The day that my body said enough is enough was the day I was given a choice to begin developing a new level of awareness and listening to my emotional and physical body's needs. I realized that by cultivating this relationship, everything I experienced was going to be more successful and more fulfilling.

The world is on autopilot and in total disconnect. We Gorge ourselves on food, watch TV's in the gym, text while we walk, or worse, text at the dinner table when sitting with friends or partners! We rush to get to yoga class on time, set impossible and meaningless deadlines, the list goes on... Breaking the disconnection means building awareness of yourself, of your environment and all the little moments that make up life.

### *Awareness as a Daily Practice*

Cultivating awareness is a process that requires us to slow down, and you may not feel anything the first couple of times you put this into practice. Our sensory perception has been bogged down by busy lives, rush hour traffic, bright lights, loud cities, living at full speed, and being out of touch with nature. That's a lot of loud stimulation to overcome, be patient with yourself. It is an unlearning process to return to the simplicity of your inner being, your reborn state.

Awareness is an artful practice with unending depths of nuance. But at its core, it is the simplest practice. Cultivating awareness is simply consciously choosing to be more present. Here's how to practice it in real life:

1. Make a conscious commitment to mentally check in with yourself throughout the day. To help create a routine choose a daily experience that will trigger the practice of self observation and awareness building. It could be when your are driving, when you are standing in line at the store, when you are on the phone with someone, or any daily experience.

2. In any time—in the grocery line waiting for check out, while you are on a business call, when you are out on a date—allow your attention to observe what your physically body is feeling in the moment.

3. Move your attention to your breath, then to different parts of your body. You will likely notice tension and by simply drawing the attention for a moment, you will be able to relax that part of your body.

It's really that simple. You are working your new awareness muscle which takes practice. Do this throughout the day and through this awareness you can have the power to change your situation in the moment.

When the body moves from tense to open and relaxed, it means communication becomes much clearer, there is more availability to connect with others, more peace and joyfulness. You also will know if you need to remove yourself from a situation based on what your body is telling you.

## Unwinding — When Tension Has No Place to Go

We are so prone to follow a continuous path forward, constantly pushing, striving, and asking ourselves what the next step should be, what the next thing is to accomplish. What is often missed on this continuous path to accomplishment is a key step called "unwinding." It means to literally pause and become empty. It means to actually do nothing and just find stillness.

Imagine a children's tire-swing spinning endlessly at the end of its rope. Eventually, when the swing has turned too far in one direction the rope gets all tight and bunched up and won't go any farther. The only way to keep it spinning is to pause, let go, and allow it to spin in the other direction. This creates an unraveling process. In a way, it is freeing up energy and making space. Once the rope is unwound, empty in a sense, the tire-swing may be spun again.

Allowing the pause, allowing the spin to happen the other way is all the creativity, energy, breath, and conscious actions coming through. Imagine you were this rope. Imagine you have been unraveled. The mind, body, energy body, and spirit have been cleared of stagnation, cleared of old remnants of stress, stories, emotional overload, and ideas. You have new space, and more capacity for all the experiences that want to come through you and to be expressed in your home, work and play!

I am not going to sit here and tell you how easy this will be. This may be very challenging at first. The body and the mind are on autopilot going over a hundred miles an hour and you are asking it to come to a dead stop. Well just like a car going that fast, if you abruptly slam on the breaks it might be catastrophic.

Once you master unwinding, the outcome is a mass amount of creativity that appears in abundant waves because you have space and capacity to accept it. You have more vitality, and centeredness. Peace returns to your experiences.

Your body naturally feels more intimately connected to people and life. You feel more. You have more deep body passion and enthusiasm to give to your lover. That's exciting! Prior to this process, so much of this energy is wasted on rushing around, being overstimulated, and working on getting things done.

You will have more to give, and in a way which adds quality to your and your loved one's lives by addressing why things are difficult in the first place. To sustainably shift what is outside us we must be nourished, strong and vital inside body, mind and spirit.

### The Need to Unwind

I remembered when I decided it was time to take my business to a whole new level. I needed to meet the right people, people who could help me in spreading my work around the world. What started out as simply joining networking groups, socializing more, grew and morphed until a year later, I was taking on more and more mass media marketing, and I started feeling drained, unsatisfied and that something was not aligning with my wellbeing. I noticed I started wanting to spend more time in my quiet place, and less time out there. When work was done, I shut my door and cut off the world because my whole being needed to rest. This was another wake up call that all too many of you may relate to.

One day I paused everything, the marketing, the networking, the meetings and I asked myself what I needed. It all came down to me making the choice that being wound up and tired was not serving me, the quality of relationships I desired and what I wanted to feel with people. It was time to unwind.

My unwinding meant hiring others such as event coordinators and personal assistants to take over for a few weeks while I got clear. When I took the break to do only those things that light my body up—breathing exercises, yoga, walks in nature, sitting at home all day just listening to the rain, sharing vulnerable talks with close friends—unwinding started to happen. Life started to talk on new life again. I began meeting the right people in an organic way because I now had genuine enthusiasm in my heart to talk to more people and I did not have to shut my door so tightly at the end of the day or force my way into introductions.

When you fly on an airplane, during the safety briefing, you are always instructed to put your oxygen mask on before you assist anyone else in putting on theirs. There is a very good reason why. If everyone is struggling to breathe and you try to help someone else before you can catch your own breath, you stand the risk of passing out. Then where would you be? Where would the person who needs your help be? If you put your mask on first, you give yourself the capacity to help others. This is true of all kinds of self care, especially unwinding. We like to think we can take care of the world without taking care of ourselves. However that is a catastrophe waiting to happen. By seeing to your own needs you increase your capacity to help others with theirs.

### Boundaries

Getting all wound up happens. Mostly it happens because you're unaware of your personal boundaries. Again and again, you may have over-committed yourself to something or someone. You may have allowed others to place their needs on your shoulders. Sometimes this is done unconsciously while at other times you are aware you agreed to something even if you whole body and mind was telling you "No!" The solution is to set and respect personal boundaries.

A boundary is a clearly formed and stated line on behaviors that create emotional, energetic and psychological harm or disharmony to your present state. Boundaries are like guidelines that create a safe atmosphere in any relationship. They create the parameters around what one's physical, mental, emotional, psychological and spiritual capacity is in regards to how they desire to be treated, met by others and what ways they are willing to show up with others.

Boundaries are permeable which means that they are not borders or solid walls. As we shift and evolve or as we get to know another our boundaries may change or shapeshift, as I like to say. You are responsible for your boundaries, for making them clear and walking away if others continuously override them.

You may think putting up a boundary is a selfish act and would keep others at a far distance. However, setting boundaries is quite the opposite. Setting a boundary is an act of love when it comes from a mindful aware place. Boundaries communicate what we are needing and feeling. Boundaries allow us to relax into being present and feel another. When you feel safe, you become more present and space opens to allows others to really know you.

Setting boundaries is a tool, an art in your ongoing unwinding process. Without you knowing your personal boundaries you become bound to everyone else's drama and get pulled around by it. Winding up, or armoring is the way the body believes it is protecting itself. Your actions reveal your deeper self, and here it means you may not yet in a place where you can take care of yourself along the way. The result is that you suffocate and start to put up a strong border.

Unwinding is simply a process of feeling safe again physically, emotionally, energetically and psychologically so your nervous system has what it needs to relax and open again.

We will continue our discussion on boundaries later on in the book once we start talking about relating to others. For now, understand that setting a boundary—setting out behaviors and actions you will not accept or engage with, both from others and from yourself—is an important part in unwinding.

### *How to Unwind*

How exciting to know unwinding is a choice within your reach! Unwinding simply means returning to your center of integrity, calming the nervous system, relaxing the muscles and mind. When you unwind you will feel more relaxed in your body, the mind will be more relaxed, clearer and any frantic underlining anxiety from a busy day will wash away.

Even though that choice may seem nearly impossible when caught up in the spin of life, my invitation to you is to just cut the cord and stop. It may feel scary but this is a necessary exploration to finally create something different within you and your relationships!

It may take putting a few logistical components into place, such as setting time and space aside in your calendar. It may also require uncovering what needs you have around the unwinding experience.

What are some of your clear boundaries and requests you would need to have a conversation about with those who share the home or work environment? What is the environment that will support this stillness and solitude? Is it the time of year, or maybe the time of day? What logistics may need to be taken care of in the days or months beforehand to ensure this quality self-love time?

I spent the months prior to my extended time of solitude

and meditation retreats gathering a team, training them, and making sure they had everything they needed in place to represent my business while I was away. I placed an ad and found a person to sublet my home. There were conversations with my partner to ensure there were no surprises or undue stress around my upcoming experience.

Remember to watch out for the Manic Mind which keeps you wound up, running in circles which takes more time in the long run. Doing things differently does not mean being less productive in your life. It is quite the opposite.

## When Joy Becomes a Choice

Life will always happen, I like to say. Things will not always go the way our minds want them to. How often have you heard that you always get what you need but it may not look like what you want? So often we attach joy to what we want. This began at such a young age. What comes to my mind is the reward system as children. You may remember this one as well. When you did something "good" that your parents approved of you received something you really wanted as a reward. You were happy and ecstatic when you received this, right!? What happened when you did something that was not approved of? When you did not get the toy, the candy, the attention you really wanted? Did you feel joy? Most likely your body felt tense, became wound up, you may have kicked and screamed because you thought life would be over without that object of your desire.

Now bring yourself to your present adult life. You have business deals that you know you have to have, relationships that make you happy, people who you need to act a certain way, but what happens when these situations don't go the way you want? Are you able to feel joy?

I am presenting a challenging idea here, and I invite you to continue with an open mind. In fact I love Frank Zappa's quote "A mind is like a parachute. It doesn't work if it is not open." I am not asking you to believe what I am saying but to rather apply these principles and practices to your own life and experience it for yourself.

True joy is something that lives within you. No person, place or thing can take this from you. Feelings happen, they are part of human nature. You will at times feel sad, disappointed, even angry, however joy will always remain. Joy does not mean you are walking around with a super smile on your face but it means within these human feelings you know deep inside that everything is going to be okay. You will eventually find the opportunity in your disappointments and find this adds life to your life.

I had a client who was brilliant at this. He owned his own company and was so excited about its success. One day he came to me sharing that he likely just lost his biggest client which, for those of you who own big companies know, can be catastrophic. Rather than looking at it like it was the end of the world, he says, "I am very disappointed and it does add a bit of stress to life right now but it means I get to find new doors that are opening." With a clear mind he came up with a clear new strategy, felt his feelings about the situation and began to see where his work was being called to serve next. He had a choice and he stayed proactive and in his place of joy. He had also extensively exercised his EQ muscle.

Life will always happen, and choosing joy is not always easy, especially when the Manic Mind, filled with old emotional chaos and stories, wants to control the situation. But I am going to invite you to dig deep here to step into your power place.

The brilliance of unwinding is having the ability to feel

joy and self fulfillment anytime. Joy becomes a choice! This is where your commitment is to your happiness, joy and wellbeing. This is going to be fuel for successful, fulfilling, passionate relationships.

# Your Emotions Are Allies

I have had more than one person say to me, "If I feel my emotions they will consume me, and I feel scared." That is an honest assessment and it's important to address it. It is important to feel those emotions, and in doing that, you must not ask yourself or you tell yourself not to feel scared. It is actually the opposite. Let yourself feel scared and investigate that feeling. Most likely the thought of being consumed is a conditioned response. So, unpack the concept of being consumed—what does it feel like and look like to be consumed?

Unattended emotions will create havoc on your relationships. They will hold onto you so tightly, you feel frozen and unable to access the level of fulfillment and connections you want in sharing your soul's purpose.

Your emotions are one of your greatest allies, and your vulnerability is absolutely attractive and sexy! Your emotions are worthy of love and understanding and you are going to share this new found love with them.

I know all too well that it can feel scary. I have been there. The morning after my physical collapse, when I woke up barely able to walk, had gained 30 pounds in 48 hours and was feeling immense physical and emotional pain, I wanted to numb myself to the world. However, we must feel something in order to create lasting change, to feel shows we are alive. My cry became "I would rather feel everything than nothing at all!" Your feelings are going to be your stepping stone to uncovering and discovering what you need. This will begin to allow you to make more empowered choices and feel more intimately connected. Using your awareness tools, you can turn your emotions into your most powerful ally.

## Your Brain on Emotions

Why is it that something can trigger us in such a way that the intensity of emotion is uncontrollable? The structure and functioning of your brain has a lot to do with this. Though this book is not the platform to unpack the science of the brain, I want to shed a little light on our biology's role in how we experience our emotions. As we develop a more in depth intimate relationship with our selves and others, it is worth acknowledging how the brain affects our life and choices.

It's important to understand how the brain can get to an emotional explosion so quickly and often over such a seemingly small trigger in order to have more compassion towards yourself and others.

There is a region of the brain called the limbic system which is made up of several parts of the brain that are generally involved in the processing and expressing of emotions. The term is limited, however, because there are various ideas of what parts of the brain should be included in the limbic system[1]. In general, the thinking part of your brain, called the cortex, maintains control over the more primitive, emotional reactions of the limbic system[2].

However, the emotional brain responds faster to events than the thinking brain. If it perceives a threat it can take over, or hijack the rest of the brain, before the thinking part has had time to analyze what is going on. That first emotional impulse

---

[1]Rob DeSalle and Ian Tattersall, *The Brain: Big Bangs, Behaviors, and Beliefs* (Yale University Press, 2012), p. 157
[2]James V. McConnell, *Understanding Human Behavior*, 5th ed. (Holt, Rinehart and Winston, 1986), 108

when something triggers you is your body being taken over by the limbic system, getting ready to fight or run. This reaction is a result of evolution (that is to say it helped keep our ancestors alive), and is supposed to be on a hair-trigger3.

The emotional part of your brain is often referred to colloquially as the reptilian part of your brain. This name comes from a theory of brain development meant to describe the successive addition of brain layers over evolutionary time called triune brain theory4. Although the divisions in the triune brain theory don't exactly overlap with the limbic system, I like the name reptilian brain because it reminds us that we are dealing with ancestral, fight or flight reactions, things that are elemental to our survival.

If the reptilian part of the brain is busy scanning for potential threats and does not have the ability to differentiate the triggers that stimulate feeling threatened from actual threats, it can wreak emotional uproar in your experiences, and in the way you relate under pressure.

Past trauma and suppressed emotions which are stored in your body memory often makes one hyper-alert to certain experiences, or rather, completely shut down and go into avoidance of the triggering experience. Emotional brain activity gets processed so quickly through the lens of past memory that if one does not have the awarenesses and tools to interrupt that process before it becomes an explosion, it can be detrimental to relating.

---

[3]Daniel Goleman, Interview by Dennis Hughes, *Share Guide,* 2004, www.shareguide.com/Golean.html

[4]Rob DeSalle and Ian Tattersall, *The Brain: Big Bangs, Behaviors, and Beliefs* (Yale University Press, 2012), 161

If you experience high anxiety from an emotional upset, the reptilian brain is quick to take control and will leave you unable to feel your feelings or identify what you need. The nervous system is much too activated.

You might have experienced this where you get upset and the upset gets worse, the arguments intensifies, the other person gets triggered and rages back. Neither of you is able to feel the deep painful feelings clearly or understand what your needs are, let alone communicate them. This is because your reptilian brain is controlling your nervous systems and emotional state.

One must address and calm the nervous system prior to having the ability to address past emotional triggers or upsets. It allows the cortex to regain its functioning, its thinking capacity. This is why throughout the book we are using tools such as breathing exercises, developing awareness and body sensitivity along with building your emotional intelligence tools so that you are more in the drivers seat than the reptilian brain.

*Vulnerability and How it's Really a Strength*

I remember Mark who signed up for mentoring in my Soulful Relating 7-Step Program. When I asked Mark what his intention or desired outcome was, he said "I want to be a better lover." I remember our first appointment and the way he presented me with a list to check off in search of his ideal mate. He was extremely analytical which was his gift, but also his hindrance. Relating to people became very structured and mechanical for him, complete with lists and agendas. The lists and agendas began to interfere with his sex life to the point that he started experiencing erectile dysfunction. It was discovered the agenda, the need to figure it all out actually was a protection mechanism hiding him from his own vulnerability.

Mark realized in our first appointment how scared he was to be vulnerable with a partner. When he and a date would begin to get all hot and ready for some sexual play his body would shut down. At first, it caused the inability to get an erection. Then it grew and morphed into the inability to communicate his true feelings, with his partner going off into their own story (an evaluation of an experience, situation or person often based on your emotional triggers). The result was separation rather than connection, and many unfulfilled nights.

As you can imagine, Mark felt ashamed and scared. His solution was to set an achievable goal using an analytical list of desires, which did not help.

Soon enough he began to talk about his fears, about feeling incompetent and not like a man, about how much shame was there. The more he opened up, the more he exposed his vulnerability, the lighter his body became. His mind let go of a need to perform, he tore up his ideal-mate checklist and began to share himself more honestly and authentically in all his interactions. All kinds of connections, even conversations with strangers, became richer. People seemed to trust him more instantly, he was more connected to life around him. By the time we had finished our 90 days of mentoring, a partner who naturally matched his values had shown up in his life ready to share at such a deep vulnerable level.

Vulnerability became this CEO's best asset. Through sharing his vulnerably in an honest and open way, he attracted other more open and emotionally matched people.

It is not easy to share your vulnerabilities, let alone believe that they make you beautiful. But when you share vulnerably with another, you invite them to truly know you and for you to know them. From this place you can co-create epic collaborations that will truly serve the personal or professional relationship and the world as a whole.

You will find, depending on the circumstance, there will be various degrees of vulnerability shared. This is natural. However, sharing vulnerability ultimately means you are being honest, clear and compassionate towards the self and another and taking ownership for your feelings along the way.

## Moving Beyond Right and Wrong — The Art of Compassion

You are now ready to begin the journey of understanding your emotions (the raw instinctive reactions based on the chemical response of the brain during a triggering experience, over which you may feel as if you have no control), as well as the actions and reactions you have to various life experiences. When we are able to move out of the judgment stage of life where we look at things from "right or wrong," and into a deep desire to understand ourselves, others, and all of our feelings underneath our stories, it opens up opportunity to deepen our relationships.

Everyone wants connection and love. That often is the reason for our fight and struggle to prove others wrong and to attack when we're upset. It seems we have been trained to fight for what we want, to prove ourselves and demand to be loved, respected and heard. However, when we fight for love, what we get is more fighting. What happens is arguments, distance and conversations that end in silently going your own way with everyone more emotionally guarded than before. Such a result can leave us to judge our negative emotions as wrong, somehow.

It can happen when we experience fear too. Typically we fear the things which we cannot control or organize—feelings, longings, loneliness, weakness, or others who are different from us. Truly nothing can be controlled and so it would seem natural for us to be comfortable accepting the flexibility and the insecurity that comes with the unknown. Yet we are not comfortable with letting go, and the endless fear of an unknown future can also leave us judging our own reaction to the unknown.

To transform anything, we must make friends with everything inside of us. Your emotions aren't good or bad, they're messengers from your emotional body intelligence letting you know it is needing something. They want to speak with you, to redirect you and let you know what this part of you needs so you can move forward. Emotions let you know what might be on or off track in your relationships or your work projects.

I have found that when I tune into this communication from within, it allows me to really listen on a subtle level to what I'm needing. It allows me to feel empathy inside myself without a need to speak it. I am also able to be honest with my needs and how flexible and available I am to get those needs met.

Are you ready to start understanding your emotional body, its triggers and upset rather than judging them as wrong? What if your emotional go-to tool here were curiosity? Every time you judge a situation or a person get curious about it. Ask yourself what you are feeling that made you come to that judgment. In this, you turn the attention away from the judgment itself and towards what caused the judgment. It's a more responsible reaction, and puts the focus where you can make an actual change.

*Radical Self Responsibility*

Self responsibility is a doorway into greater freedom. On an emotional level it means taking ownership of your thoughts, feelings, words and actions.

We have been conditioned throughout our lifetimes to give away responsibility to another when it comes to our emotional needs and even some physical needs. The problem is that it means along your lifetime there is going to be an overwhelming amount of tiresome disappointments. Your dependency on another means that that other person has some extraordinary power over your reality.

I am not saying that someone having extraordinary power over your reality is necessarily a bad thing, however taking responsibility for your own emotional and physical needs can greatly add to the quality of your life. You will breathe easier and really have joy in life, and in the relationships that fuel it.

We live in a world where each individual has their own emotional past. Lives are made up of different stories which create the present day personalities. There are so many different views, people making different choices, having different values, likes and dislikes.

Who am I to say my choices would serve another better than their own choices, or to put someone else in that place to be responsible for my life and ultimately my happiness? That would lead to a miserable life, wouldn't it?

I spoke about joy being a choice earlier in the book. This is relevant in this topic because when you choose to be self responsible your joy is always there.

When you are being self responsible, you:
- Show up present in the moment. Self responsibility begins with awareness.

- Understand, acknowledge and feel your feelings.
- Take ownership of your feelings and your actions honestly.
- Be proactive and communicate your feelings from the "I" perspective without blaming.

I was at a business networking event once and sitting at a table with a group of women sharing stories and about ourselves. The woman next to me looked at me and asked "Are you alway this calm?" also noting how present I was. When she asked I giggled and told her she should ask my partner at the time. I too have my storms and life also happens as we are all perfectly human. I went on to share with her that no matter what level of calm we seem to have, the situations that we judge as stressful will not stop happening. But that in finally taking ownership for ourselves and our roles in those stressful situations and our reactions to them, we develop the skills to gracefully navigate life no matter what the circumstances.

## Friends in the Closet

Imagine there is a closed door, and your mind is warning you that whatever is behind it is off limits. But you know that behind that door, there is another door for you to discover. Imagine too, that all those feelings of sadness, anger, frustration, envy, jealousy, rage, grief and joy are people just like you. Yes, let's imagine they are people or old friends even. And they have a voice and a purpose. Imagine that all those emotions, those people are captive behind that second closed door. You go through the first door, into the anteroom of powerful emotions. When you open that second door, whatever, whoever is inside will be cinfined here with you.

So, all those emotions that have been held captive in the

forbidden closet, at one time were your friends that you explored life with. But then, something happened and somewhere along the way you did not like what they were saying. You resisted them and began to fight against what they were telling you. Then one day you had enough and couldn't take it anymore, so you shoved them in the closet, locked the door, and lost the key.

WOW! Well, I know how I would feel if my friend shoved me in a closet and lost the key! I would do whatever I could to get out. I would start to yell loudly and bang on the door in hopes someone would hear me and come to my rescue. Now imagine if you were the one locked in that closet. Well, guess what? You are! You have locked away parts of yourself in that forbidden closet. Important parts. Parts that used to be your friends.

Your mind has appointed itself the warden that has held your emotions as prisoners. Your mind's intention was to protect you from harm by encouraging you to run in the other direction, hoping that if enough time passed those parts of you would eventually disappear.

My question to you is, did it work? Have all those unwanted feelings gone away? Or, have you simply done your best to forget them?

We have all done it; wanting to escape with aspirations of experiencing something different, perhaps better or, at least, more pleasant. Yet over time, those feelings weigh us down, leaving us feeling heavy and disconnected because they didn't go away. We were never taught how to embrace, face, and most importantly understand and actually befriend these parts of ourselves, our feelings. We have been taught to judge them, to withhold and not express them. It wasn't safe for others to see us feeling like that. We were taught that some feelings were not okay, that they were bad, scary and unacceptable.

When you begin to work with you emotions they start to be on the same team with you. They will root for your success in your relationships. They understand that they don't have to be so dramatic to get your attention. That means they will empower your relationships, your relationship choices. Your partner and loved ones will even feel more attracted to you. They will feel safer because you will become more available. Now that's exciting!

You may be wondering what you are to do with all these new or perhaps old feelings. Most likely, you aren't sure what to do. Your mind is telling you not to open the closet door because it is dark and scary. It warns you that it is unsafe to go in there, reminding you that, "You don't have a clue of what will happen if you open that door!" Your mind flashes a bright, neon warning light to stay away from the danger that lurks behind that closet door. Then it attempts to distract you with temptation. It reassures you that there is more fun in another direction. But you must invite those emotions in if you are going to turn them into the powerful allies they can be.

### Using Leverage

I'm going to give you some tools to use when you are exploring your emotional body. You can use these tools any time, including when something unexpected happens that stirs up strong emotions in you. But first, I want you to try an exercise.

It is quite natural for resistance to arise in your mind when emotions and uncomfortable feelings begin to move and make themselves known. And it's quite natural to resist exploring those emotions. The biggest key in assisting you in these moments is to remembering your leverage. We spoke about leverage earlier when talking about setting up a daily practice.

Go back and review the section if you need to.

Today's Exercise is deconstructing your story, so you can uncover what you are feeling and needing. I want you to recall a recent interaction with someone when you felt yourself going into defense mode. That might look like wanting to overly explain yourself, proving you are right and the other is wrong, or blaming another so you look good. Observe and notice if, during your interaction, you were trying hard to get what you wanted and to have the other person see your side of the story. Notice that the harder you tried, the less understanding you would get. You were met with resistance, which caused you and others stress.

How do we deconstruct and break down the Manic Mind and emotional story? We must read between the lines to find out! Your next steps are to think back and answer the following questions:

- What was I truly feeling? For example, I was feeling sad, frustrated, angry, helpless, etc. (Look at the Universal Human Feelings List to assist you in getting clarity.)
- What story did I tell myself about this situation? Remember a story is the emotional evaluation you give a situation based on your upset and trigger. The story is often based on blaming and making others responsible for our feelings. For example, they did this to me, this is their fault I feel _____, How dare they treat me like this?!?
- What was I needing? (Look at the Universal Human Needs chart to assist you in identifying what you are needing.) For example, I was needing acknowledgment, appreciation, affection, solo time.
- How could I have effectively and with self responsibility (taking ownership for what emotions you are feeling

rather than pointing the finger and blaming), let the other person know what I was feeling and needing?

When you discovered what you were feeling and needing, were some of these discoveries unwelcome? Did they cause you some agitation or perhaps congestion in your body? Were you surprised by some unexpected feelings that surfaced and came into awareness? Notice that when you reflect on the situation now, there is more clarity, there is more room for new feelings, room to move on. Finally, ask yourself, what has not feeling my emotions given me? You must be able to feel sadness in order to feel joy. When you block pain you also block pleasure.

### *Exploring Your Emotions*

I'd like to give you a couple of tools you can use to explore your emotional body. The first is a mindfulness tool I like to use to make myself present. If I am getting caught up in emotional drama and the "old stuff" I make a point of getting really present. Here's how to do that:

1. look around you at your physical location, and ask am I safe in the environment? Most likely the answer is yes.
2. Get still, sit if possible, but most importantly invite breath into your diaphragm. Review the breath exercise in earlier chapters if necessary.
3. Get present to your surroundings and take a mental note of what you see. I see a tree, I see clouds, I see a television. Make note of what is in your nearby environment.
4. Get present to the sensations you are feeling in your body, not your label or judgment of them but go right to the sensation. This is a physiological response.

These four easy steps are a simple way to detach from the old emotional story that you are unsafe.

Remember this is not a replacement for counseling or mentoring from a professional but tools to keep your home practices on track.

The second tool is very similar to the exercise you tried above about deconstructing your story. In fact, it's pretty much the same, only you use it in the moment rather than after the fact.

When you go into an experience, overhear a conversation, hear something which is upsetting, use this tool to discover what about the experience is actually your own story and assumptions. Get still and answer these questions:

1. What am I feeling? Sad, disappointed, etc.
2. What is the story I am telling myself about this situation?
3. Can I know for certain my story is true?
4. What am I needing?

From here we each take ownership for our feelings and needs. As well, now we have fueled our emotional intelligence and have the ability to be proactive in communicating and asking for further information, for clarity and to be present enough for another perspective. In a coming chapter you will learn how to take that new intelligence about your emotional state and effectively communicate it to whomever you're interacting with.

## When Intense Feelins Arise

Today I am going to invite you to pause right there. Pay attention the moment you see that flashing warning light. Instead of running away, notice your body's sensations, as it begins to freeze or prepares for the fight or flight. Notice how the primitive reptilian brain has taken over.

Yes, I am asking you to pause in that most uncomfortable and perhaps foreign experience for a moment. Now you may be wondering, "Is this woman absolutely out of her mind?" And the right answer would be a resounding, "Yes! I am out of mind; I am in my heart."

Today is the day you clear the way to finding a new path into your heart. I know it may feel uncomfortable, even a bit scary. It is something unknown, untested. That is a very common experience at first. The unknown can be scary. Yet, I am inviting you to trust me as your alchemist guide, who would like to show you how to transmute fear into enthusiasm and excitement with a simple shift of perspective.

As you continue on this journey, you will find that the more you are able to welcome, embrace and understand powerful feelings, the more you will develop the capacity to be present and understanding with yourself and those you relate to in life. You will feel safer with them and they will feel safer with you.

How, you might ask, do we make this shift from fear into love? My answer is that it begins by unlocking the door and being courageous enough to peek inside that closet. You have started the process already by completing the exercise in the last chapter. You learned a lot about yourself in that process. Now there is space for you to see, feel and explore the most powerful emotions in your emotional body, negative and positive.

You might ask "what if I feel hate? What if I am in such a state of rage and anger that to sit in it seems impossible?" The impossible part is your fight or flight signal saying "Danger, danger." However, if you practice the exercises in the section on cultivating awareness, you will have a way to get a few breaths in. Your breath will be your biggest ally.

I have felt hate before. We often think we hate a person when we may be mad or when something is not going the way we really had wanted. However, what truly is happening is that we hate the choices that the other is making and that part of us which is so sad wants to use hate as a way to protect our vulnerabilities. I Most recently felt hate when my partner and I transitioned our relationship. I felt such grief and sadness but I also felt rage and anger and I so wanted to hate him. I had to come face to face with my feelings before their grip on me finally softened and I could feel safe enough to let go of control, or let go of the control they had over me.

There are some basic tools for dealing with powerful, uncomfortable emotions. They may seem rather simple, however during a trigger, using these tools may be the most challenging thing to remember.

Creating a break-state is what is required in these moments to shake you out of the emotional trap. To do this:

1. Pause, and bring you breath into your lower belly. When we are triggered and caught in an emotional loop, the breath often gets contracted, tight and stuck in the throat and chest.

2. Shake your body and make sound.

3. Get outside. Go walk in nature, swim in a lake or take yourself to a yoga class. What these actions have in common is they require you to be more in your body and less in your head. They all calm the nervous system and often elevate peace and joy. Once you are in this clearer state you can revisit the situation from a clearer perspective.

*Getting In Touch With Powerful Positive Feelings*

We are the poets who write our own stories. We are the magicians who have the ability to see inside the mystery. We are the artists who are able to create masterpieces in every moment. Powerful feelings play an important role in fueling our inner artists, and today I invite you to focus on the powerful feelings, on what juices you up. Place yourself in the places that you feel plugged in, surround yourself with the people or conversations which lift you up. It is important to be able to tap into this rich inner resource whenever you need to.

We have a lot of assumptions about powerful feelings, so it's important to be truthful with yourself about what really is your fuel. Watch out and notice how sometimes we may choose an experience because it seems exciting and everyone is doing it. Yet you feel empty, drained and unclear afterwards. This is a good sign that you have stepped out of that which resonates with your joy, your passion and your highest place of vitality.

Each day is an opportunity to choose what excites your whole being. You know when you feel your whole body say YES! Listen to the body wisdom and feelings pulsating and speaking to you. I know when I am plugged in and listening I get juiced up and clear about everything else around me. My relationships and life simply flow in ease and connection when I am tuned in.

Here are a few easy steps to find out where you are over-committing and what truly fuels your joy and passion.

Create two lists on paper. In one column list activities, situations and places in which you feel clear, centered and juiced up. In the other column write down activities, perhaps relationships and events that cause you to feel in some way de-energized, unclear, chaotic and drained afterward. Now watch and listen. Don't try to fix anything. Just look at what ignites a fire within you to live a more juicy life.

There is no right or wrong. This is merely an experiment of observation. Pay attention to how you feel in each situation.

Be present and aware, even if it is unpleasant or uncomfortable because you will learn something about yourself from the experience. This exercise is about feeling rather than judging how well you do or don't like something. There are many things we like to do that simply may not be aligning with the direction we want to go in life. It isn't necessarily about liking something or feeling good about it that ignites us.

Create boundaries for yourself. Choose from the first column how many times per week you need to engage in those activities and be with the people or in the places that empower you to feel plugged in. You must allow yourself those things because allowing them in your life supports everything else in your life and relationships. Then choose how often you will tolerate or choose not to experience the items in the column that depletes, drains or disconnects you from your fire within.

After writing your lists, create a new page to explore and try out new boundaries and commitments to yourself to refer back to as a reminder. If you are a visual person, hanging a poster that represents what ignites the fire within you could serve as a reminder of what you get to wake up to each morning. Then create your own ritual of letting go of what drains and disconnects you so you can create more space for what energizes your life, path and relationships. I like to burn the paper which I originally wrote on as a way of allowing the energy to be burned back into ashes. For me it symbolizes recycling that energy back into the earth to be used as fertilizer to plant new seeds.

Some of us need time alone. For me, I need time alone in nature to feel juiced up and centered. Being in nature regenerates me. I even make a commitment to myself of having a minimum of at least one1 day of silence each week. During these days of sacred solitude, I don't answer my phone or have conversations with others. I go out to nature and find someplace where it is quiet. Maybe I hike or sit, meditate, read or journal. Along these lines, I also have a commitment to myself to limit weekly social activities to two groups per week maximum. I need that boundary with my full schedule and all the events and space holding I provide in my work with others. I know if I choose more, even though they are tempting and fun, it is not serving the integrity of my relationships or work. I create a balance for myself so everything flows in harmony.

Bottom line: remember to have fun! Get out there and get juiced up! Remember that the more you take time out to discover yourself, the more you will learn to honor yourself, which will expand your capacity for more intimacy in relationships and life.

## The Art of Deep Listening with Oneself

You are guaranteed that everything you have avoided in your emotional life will eventually jump out in front of you calling for your attention.

When we want to have a candid conversation with a friend, it is important we create a sense of safety and have a warm, clear, comfortable space to meet them. Make sense? Then imagine that all those uncomfortable feelings you used to avoid and lock away are now long lost buddies who have come to visit. And all they really want from you is to be loved, seen and acknowledged, just like you want to be loved, heard and understood. The key to getting out of reacting and judging and into understanding is to truly listen. We are going to develop the sense of Deep Listening, something you will apply to others, and also to yourself.

So, for example, imagine your old friend Anger comes

knocking on your front door. And, even though Anger isn't necessarily the politest and most pleasant guest to have around (he might even make the other guests uncomfortable as he is feeling stressed out), you invite Anger into your living room. You now have the capacity to do this because of the work you've done in dealing with powerful emotions. It helped you gain clarity and get centered. Your head may say, "What, are you crazy? Danger! What are you doing?" But I invite and encourage you to stay in your heart and show Anger some love by being present with him.

Now that you have invited Anger in, you observe him and allow him to adjust to his new surroundings. At first he looks at you with this scolding look, arms clenched in front of him. You simply notice and continue to be a good hostess. You offer Anger something to drink to help him feel welcome. Then Anger, and his buddies who are waiting outside peering in, start to shift from rigidness to curiosity. Anger steps one foot through the door, wanting to come in, yet still a bit hesitant. You bring him a warm cup of tea, turn on some light music and look at him and his buddies waiting outside.

You ask Anger, "How may I support you right now?" Anger and his pals begin to tremble with nervousness. To be treated like this, to be welcomed, not rejected, is so foreign to them. They are so surprised that you are still there with them. They thought for sure you would have run away, like all the other times in past experiences. But you are still here so Anger is feeling safer now. He is surprised at the strong desire to be closer that is developing within him. So Anger cautiously enters the living room, relieved that it is so much warmer and more comfortable than the closet he had been trapped in for so many years. Slowly Anger continues to make his way across the room, with his friend Nervousness, to the comfortable cushions on the floor. You follow Anger and offer him a blanket. Then you sit down across from him. At this point, Anger is rather confused by such unexpected hospitality. As you continue to be present, kind and caring, Nervousness watches close by.

Anger's strategy has always been to push people away by scaring them off. Yet you are no longer scared of Anger. You look at Anger and gently ask again, "What do you need from me? Why are you so angry?" At that moment, something begins to happen. Anger has never experienced such presence, care, and attention. Nervousness realizes she doesn't have to protect her friend Anger anymore and allows Sadness to join Anger in the room. Now, you have now been introduced to a group of friends. Anger, Fear, Nervousness, and Sadness, who all feel safe to be sitting in the living room with you. You are pleasantly surprised to notice that the more present you are with them, the calmer they become. And, because they trust you and feel safe and calm with you now, they reward you for your patience and presence by revealing to you the answers you seek with their transparency. Deep Listening finds the wisdom contained in our emotions. You must start your Deep Listening journey by first listening to yourself. Incorporate Deep Listening into your daily breath practice.

Deep Listening involves all the components of breath, awareness and presence as they all increase your ability to feel more of what is happening in your body both physiologically and emotionally.

Deep Listening means beginning to bring all your attention to all parts of yourself from moment to moment to feel what is alive for you, what the body is needing in the moment. When we don't deeply listen often the choices we make don't match what a deeper aspect of us wants or needs. How often have you said yes to doing something and the entire time you felt a knot in your solar plexus or you held you breath? That was the body and emotional body talking to you and you weren't listening.

I remember when I was going through some pretty huge relationship changes with my partner. We had consciously chosen to transition our relationship (You will learn more about that later in the book.) It meant things were shifting in how we expressed ourselves with each other.

We were living together at the time and had been in a deep, rich, extraordinary partnership for three and a half years. You may imagine the emotions that come up when such a relationship needs to change. The mourning, the grief, the sadness, and yes the anger, even moments of rage.

My emotions were in full-on conversation with me and in order for me to hear them I needed to pause, get still and engage in Deep Listening. These, you could imagine, were very challenging circumstances to get still in. I felt so sad and my sense of stability, which came from outside factors—my home and my relationship—was crumbling. My personal motto is that life is always inspiring in our favor. It will push us out of the nest when it is time. Sometimes it means changes in relationships, ending relationships or career paths. Though that does not deny the human fact of feelings.

It is important to note that with the big changes the nervous system becomes overloaded, and we may feel much more sensitive. So, in order to really listen to myself, I took these steps:

- I Created a supportive environment, a place to be quiet and reflect in nature.
- I made sure to have regular communication with my partner.
- I found a few close friends and family who were able to be present without giving advice or putting their

emotional past onto my situation. I had regular support calls with them. Speaking your truth out loud to another can force you to listen to yourself.

- I journaled, asking and recording, sometimes a few times a day, what am I feeling and what am I needing?
- I kept up with my daily meditation, breath work processes, body work sessions—all things that uplift me.
- I tried to find where the doors were opening. For me it meant writing for two books, traveling to places where I felt really connected to myself; it meant engaging again globally to build a new teaching tour.

By creating this space and listening to my emotions I was able to gradually and gently move through this relationship transition feeling more empowered and more connected with my partner in a new way. He was able to stay present and committed to recreating our rich friendship.

Remember all the tools we have developed to work with our emotional bodies. All of these tools contain some kind of Deep Listening skills within them. Deep Listening is rooted in awareness; it shows us our vulnerabilities and how to turn them into strengths; it helps us move beyond right or wrong and into understanding; it helps us discover and deal with our most powerful emotions, good and bad. Deep Listening will help you come to fully know your own self, your needs and desires. And, later in the book, we will see how Deep Listening helps you come to know another.

*Coming to Know Your Own Needs and Desires*

In this exercise, I invite you to put aside 15 to 30 minutes to get to know parts of yourself in a new way, parts that you have been hiding, and to discover what your own most urgent needs and desires are.

Set up a sacred space where you will not be interrupted. Gather a pen and notebook, a glass of water, and a blanket if you think you'll need one. Prior to this moment you have been focusing on diaphamatic breathing. Bringing the breath deeper into the belly. Today another step is going to be added. You will begin to connect the inhale and exhale like a full circle or a wave.

To do the full circular connected breath:

1. Lay on an incline with your back and head fully supported.
2. Breathe in and out through the mouth.
3. Your inhale should take three times as long as your exhale, which should be completely relaxed.
4. Make you exhale like a silent sigh. Think of snapping a rubber band, how quickly it will go across the room. That is your exhale and diaphragm.
5. Connect the inhale and exhale like a circle without pausing.
6. Let go and enjoy the journey!

When you begin full circular connected breathing, place your hands on your lower belly and bring in a couple of diaphragmatic breaths. Connect the breath for at least five minutes.

After 5 minutes pick up your pen and paper. Make a list of the places from your life that you have judged and run from. Make a list of things such as your sexual desires or emotional needs that you have pushed down and felt shame around.

Get still again, review your list and start to identify what feelings you have about this list, such as sadness, anger, rage. What is your physical body feeling as well?

Identify one to three basic needs that you have on account of that list. For example, I may not have been held or felt my parents around much as a child. My need may be, I needed to be held more, I needed my parents to spend more time with me. Or, I need to communicate and speak up more as an adult, I need to surround myself with people who are open to listening, I need more conscious touch, I need to slow down when engaging sexually…

Affirm by saying out loud and writing down "I deserve _____." for every need you stated.

Close your eyes, feel and come back to your circular breathing for five minutes.

Create one step you will take today or tomorrow that will assist you in creating the life you desire with more intimacy, connection and sexual depth.

# Your Relationship to Your Sex

Your relationship with your sexuality is like a dance, and you will benefit by learning to trust this part of yourself. Sexuality is magic, an unspoken language that deserves reverence, understanding, Deep Listening, voice, expression and your personal presence. When you pay the right attention to it, your sexuality becomes an awesome communication conduit to your most authentic self.

Our sexual energy is a creative life force, a fuel that births not just babies, but anything we desire to create in our world. When harnessed, this energy has the powerful potential to be our creative fuel in our life, our projects, our relationships, our art, our writing, our love. It powers and fuels our creativity in so many realms outside the bedroom, it is what life is literally birthed from.

Harnessing your sexual energy involves a combination of practices, using your breath and consciously redirecting the energy you feel when you are turned on to focus on other creative projects. Sometimes it even means choosing not to ejaculate or orgasm during your shared or solo sexual experiences. Have you noticed feeling tired after you ejaculate, unfocused and somewhat stupid even? So just imagine if this were redirected. Your sexual experiences would be prolonged and you creativity would increase. Another way to harness that energy is turning masturbation into self pleasure—a mindful, holistic way of masturbation—which we will get to further on in this chapter. Self pleasure becomes a means to intensify, build your sexual fire and harness it when not released. You are redirecting your raw desire.

Personally, I noticed if I have a big book project or am writing a course, so much of my creative, raw, sexual energy is going in that direction that I don't feel the need for physical sex.

What's more, our sexual selves, our sexual histories hold an immense amount of information, wisdom, and experience to learn from. Seekers who have been exploring conscious sexuality as a spiritual practice believe just that! There are many practices which sense that sex and relationships have the potential to provide a deep experience of connection and the inter-connectedness of all beings and things.

So you can see there are many reasons to get to know your sexual self outside of actually having sex with someone. And until we deeply, intimately know ourselves, we will not be able to hold another is this way or have another hold us in such a way.

So, in a world where we are so busy and often are conditioned to be losing touch with feelings, vulnerability and connection, slowing down provides a safe space for us to open up and explore those feelings again. Let us slow down and explore all that wonderful inner wisdom.

### *The Way Your Sexuality Began*

How did your relationship to sex and sexuality begin? People aren't taught as children about the potential and the sheer bigness of their sexuality. It is a force that fuels everything we do; it is our life-force. When we build a relationship with it, we tend to have a healthier more liberated experience with our sex, our yearnings, our passions. If it is pushed under the carpet, treated as evil or something that only gets acknowledged behind closed doors, it often comes to control our lives, and in the process, leads us to use sexuality to manipulate the world around us in harmful ways.

Exploring my personal sexual evolution takes me back to when I was ten years old when my menstrual cycle began, to the heavy blood flow and extreme physical and emotional pain that came with it. This was the beginning of learning about who I was as a sensitive sexual being. So often this stage of life for a young woman or young man is overlooked.

My parents were divorced or newly separated at the time. I remember being with my father out for breakfast at a small town restaurant. It was morning, most likely on a Sunday because I spent the weekends with Dad. I remember suddenly feeling so much physical pain and cramping, and a very heavy cycle starting on that day. This was the beginning of some big changes in my body and no one ever sat me down to talk to me about the emotions, the physical discomfort and the feelings that would come along with it, and would only grow from this day forward.

So often children are left to figure things out for themselves. Fortunately, that seems to be changing as children are being raised with greater awareness. They are being taught about the earth, to eat more natural foods, and to communicate differently. They are are being given more of a voice. When I was ten years old things were not so open. I can image though, being as sensitive as I was, how it might have been considerably easier if I'd had the environment to help me understand my body, my emotions and my sexuality on a bigger scale.

You would think this stage of life would be taught to you as a child, yet there are still so many negative thoughts about sex based on fear, that this discussion is usually pushed under the carpet. You would also think that as we become adults, we would receive better messages about our sexuality and come to understand it better. But this is not the case either.

## *Sexual Expectations*

You see on the big screen, in magazines, in pornography and in all of the societal expectations around the sexual self, an expectation of what your own personal sexual expression and sex life should look like. What do you do if your relationship with your sexuality or desires and turn-on's don't seem to fit what society may call the norm? Many who come to me for mentoring share things about their sexuality they have not known how to share with others in their life. There is fear of judgment, of scaring their partners away or being condemned.

You may notice times when you're not feeling your sexual drive, you don't desire what others desire, you're tired of conforming to gender expectations or you really enjoy some particular kink that the world around you does not understand. In these moments it is so important to recognize what is actually someone else's idea of normal, and to address all the emotional patterns which have been created from a lifetime of feeling that you had to live up to someone else's standards. (which, of course, is not true. You don't have to live up to someone else's sexual expectations or standards!)

Now you are remembering who you are and at this stage realizing the only way to have the intimacy and connection you desire is to get real and to celebrate who you are, especially your sexual preferences and desires.

You might think, yeah but if I do this my life will fall apart. If I stop conforming people will be scared of me, I will loose my friends, my partner may run away. I am going to share some tough love with you here and ask you a question.

Would you rather live half dead, unknown, suffocating your unique gifts and surrounded by people who encourage your suffocation or would you rather breathe again, give people and loved ones a chance to know you, really know you, and begin attracting life, situations and people who encourage your uniqueness to shine? Part of that is being sexually liberated. This chapter is about discovering who that authentic non-suffocated self is. In a later chapter we will look at sex for more-than-one, which is where that person gets expressed.

I had a client who was in a relationship where his partner at the time had developed cancer and became very sick. This distanced them both emotionally and physically. My client still had sexual desire and longed for connection again. In private they turned to porn. However, over time what had happened is they lost that intimate sensitivity. Emotionally they became confined and contracted longing for human touch again but unable to completely become physically aroused in such experiences. They developed so much shame around desiring the porn in the first place, around having to keep it hidden behind closed doors that they went so far down the rabbit hole of emotions they felt trapped and lonely.

My client's Manic Mind had taken over, their body physiology followed. Lack of human contact and over-stimulation of the brain through pornography became the conditioned norm.

During our first meeting they felt so much shame when they spoke about the inability to get an erection when with a partner. They were frantic with self judgment, assuming there was something wrong with them. The moment I looked my client in the eyes and asked "who cares if you get an erection? Is your excessive need to perform and get that erection keeping you from being present and feeling the pleasure of the moment?" Their eyes widened as they looked back at me, they exhaled and completely relaxed, laughing.

They said these words were the biggest gift they could have ever received. They felt a huge weight drop off their shoulders.

"Yes," they said, "I am rarely present, and rarely feel pleasure of the moment because I always think I need to be a certain way or perform a certain way."

I went on to ask them, without that thought, did they feel the pleasure of the moment. They closed their eyes, pondered while breathing and said yes. Their expectations and agenda to perform sexually had become a capacious hiding ground for their vulnerability. They were sad and lonely yet did not want to feel it.

So here's the thing, the story I shared is certainly a multi-faceted story. There are many layers to address but the importance for the client was that they became present enough to feel again, to let go of some of the expectations. From there we were able to continue the work. From this place they could begin to understand with compassion why they made choices in their life and what new choices would really serve their highest good.

### Tending Your Sacred Fire

Your sexual energy is birthed right within you. No other is responsible for your sexual energy, nor are they responsible for your sexual turn-on or orgasm. This means that you must take responsibility for your own sexual life both with and without a partner. You must learn and discover what you need out of a sex life, and the way you do that is through meditation and mindful masturbation, which I call self pleasure.

In many cultures, there are fire keepers, those who build, watch and keep a fire healthy, alive and burning during various gatherings, ceremonies and rituals. This fire is an analogy for the fire inside each of us. Deep in the root of our bodies, our bellies, lives our sexual energy. A kind of fire and passion that produces our creative energy source or our sex.

Many people approached me after what I call "sexual awakenings." Sexual awakenings may happen after a lifetime, or several years of suppressing various emotions and judgments around one's own sexuality. Due to these suppressions and restrictions, people are living in a state where their life force energy and sexual energy flows at a lower rate, similar to what happens when a fire does not get enough oxygen. These individuals have stopped breathing, and their fire has lost its fuel.

When one begins to breath more, clear through the emotional body, one naturally begins to feel more alive, vibrant and turned on. Often this means a resurgent flow of abundant sexual energy and love. The newness of all the feelings and emotions that come along with this energy may be overwhelming, and can leave you feeling unsure of which direction to turn. Many sexual awakenings are accompanied by feelings of confusion, neediness, resistance, and shame, yet there is a powerful new joy in knowing this awakening is something so meaningful.

In a culture that has lost touch with nature it is important to remember your sexuality is first and foremost your responsibility. Society doesn't talk about this, and it treats that sacred fire as if it were unimportant when it is your fuel, your creativity, your very power. Many abuse that fire simply by ignoring it.

Fire needs the right balance of air, fuel, space, and attention to burn well. Otherwise it burns out or burns everything in sight. Remember this when thinking of your own sexuality and your relationship with it.

## *Mindfulness and Self Pleasure*

Meditative states can enhance one's ability to feel pleasure and arousal. It is where one becomes so still to observe to fill, to open, and allow life and spirit to fully enter them. Now you may be saying, if I feel turned on or aroused why not just find someone to have sex with? I am all for expressing one's sexuality, but we want sustainable, quality living, loving and relationships with our bodies, emotions and others. The aim is not to live disconnected, with shame, resentments and momentary explosions of pleasure.

Self pleasuring is a place of profound communion where we allow the mind to rest and the heart to awaken. The doing becomes being and our creative life force and sexual energy are allowed to communicate through us in the stillness. In expressing our sexuality and sharing it with others immediately, we don't tap into the fullness of where the juice flows. This is accessed deep inside of ourselves.

I find that when I am meditating, and the nervous system is at peace, I can begin to feel the states of flow, I can feel contraction, and I can feel that we are also always feeling a slight arousal state.I would describe this as subtle, gentle flowing energy currents, running through the body. Those currents make you aware of the root: your sexual center. They soften your heart and open your mind.

As activation happens in your sexual energy it activates shifts in your body chemistry, in your emotional body, in your thought processes. How you respond is more information. Do you resist it, do you contract or do you melt into what is happening? Your reaction is how your sexual self is communicating through feeling. The deeper you listen and pay attention the more you will learn about yourself, the way you relate and the unique flow of your own sexual energy.

Just as meditation is a sexual act, masturbation is a meditative act. The art and concept of self pleasure is about taking the time and being present to feeling all of the smallest and biggest sensations during an experience whether it be a self massage or sexual arousal. A key component of this is slowing down. The more we feel by slowing down the more intimately engaged we will be in the moment.

My work has shown me that people who self pleasure, are more likely to have fulfilling sex lives, better health, happier relationships and an overall increase in self confidence. You become the expert of your own body and learn to be erotically self sufficient.

Think of yourself giving someone a massage, a friend or lover. When you do this you want to be as present with how you are touching them, to the way their skin feels, to the response of their body. That is what makes for a wonderful massage. Well, the same is true when massaging yourself. You will not mindlessly knead your body while staring off at the TV or day dreaming about your next appointment. You want to pay attention and lose yourself in all the sensations that the body begins to feel when you massage it. How would you want to be met by your lover? How would you want to express yourself to your partner intimately, sensually, lovingly? Why would we expect another to show up like this, touch us like that, do this for us if we aren't able or willing to do this for ourselves?

*Self Pleasuring*

This exercise is about returning to an initmate relationship with your pleasure. In this room we will explore various aspects of self-touch, breathing, presence, and moving consciousness and awareness to different parts of your body, all in a journey through self pleasuring as a meditation. What is your body feeling in this moment? Do you feel nervousness, contraction, resistance to the thought of self pleasure as a meditation? What are your judgments around receiving pleasure, giving yourself the gift of pleasure?

Where masturbation is often associated with a quick release and getting off mindlessly, self pleasure meditations are about learning to feel more, ride waves of pleasure, learn how you like to be touched, exploring the body with presence for an extended period of time. There is no goal to orgasm or ejaculate. There is not even a goal to touch your genitals. Yet it is open for orgasm, ejaculation and touching your entire body. This is about loving your body!

Ask yourself these questions:

- Do you know how you really liked to be touched?
- Do you believe that spirituality, mindfulness and sexuality are linked?
- How vulnerable do you allow yourself to be during sex?
- How aware of yourself are you while you are sexually aroused?

These questions are simply inquiries to trigger new awarenesses, to identify where you may stop yourself from experiencing deep intimacy with another (even though we are focusing on your self relationship at the moment). If you are unable to be fully, deeply intimate with yourself, why would another meet you in such a way?

To self pleasure consciously:

1. Create time for yourself! Time where you won't be disturbed as if you are creating a date with a lover or partner. Put on some music, light some candles, use your favorite massage oil, or whatever creates a nourishing experience for you.

2. Breathe. Breath is your number one way to accelerate pleasure and presence. In life people let their Manic Minds take over, and end up holding their breath often so as not to feel. As a result, when we do become aroused our breathing becomes more shallow. When we hold our breath during sexual pleasure all the arousal remains in the genitals. Today the intention is to allow pleasure and sensation to move through the whole body without a goal. Remember the circular breath you have been practicing daily. Allow the breath to be slow, deep and relaxed. Imagine the breath as a pump circulating your energy and sensations of turn-on through your whole body. With conscious breathing we create space to receive more pleasure.

3. Be your own pleasure detective! Explore your whole body and discover those juicy spots. Be curious, as if on an adventure of your own body. Notice the places of pleasure, how you like to be touched and how it changes from place to place. Again, when you ask lovers to explore your body it is important to do the same.

4. Let any feelings, sensation of pleasure or energy activating to simply ebb and flow. When we feel arousal or sensations which feels good we usually focus on building it, heading for the goal. However arousal naturally rises and falls like the waves in the ocean. It is in riding each wave that pleasure builds, prolongs and becomes a state of being rather than a quick blissed out moment.

5. Slow down and savor your pleasure.

6. Focus on the sensations. With so much external stimulus in the world the sensations you actually are able to feel within the body may be limited. People have become

desensitized. Draw your attention to your body. How does your body feel? What sensations do you notice? Breathe. Over time with more explorations like this, you will increase the feeling, awareness and sensations in your body, which will heighten your experience when with you partner or lover. More of you to be shared and enjoyed!

Sexuality is magic, it is creative, it is life force and it is calling us to listen.

# Cleaning House — Your Body Temple

Look at your body as a temple, a house. Do you keep your house cluttered, filled with yesterday's dirty dishes, covered in emotional soot? Are people hanging out in your home that are not really caring for it? What does your internal home look like? Today we are going to set the record straight and start fresh. We are going to create a new reality that empowers you to trust and make friends with your feelings. Today we will begin to pave a new path, which you may never have walked on before. Today we are going to clean our internal house!

A clean home brings relaxation and ease. It brings presence so you can peacefully respond to others.

During the house cleaning and rearranging of the furniture, old trash, debris and perhaps old crumbs from yesterday's sandwich or even some dust mites hiding out are cleared. These are analogies for all those lurking emotions and hidden stories from the past.

All the work you've done before this moment has had to do with getting to know the depth of yourself, and exploring the challenges, edges, joys and sorrows your past has saddled you with. In a sense, before this chapter you have been exploring your life story. You have explored it in such a way that you already have begun to rewire old limiting patterns, ideas that may not be fully serving the present you anymore.

You have been pulling up the old weeds of conditioned beliefs that had you programmed to point the finger, project your agenda, make another responsible for your thoughts, actions and emotional uproars up until this point. You are now realizing how much energy, how much of your wisdom and power this was giving away. As well as how damaging a way of living this was to you, your life and relationships. From this moment forward you are going to reject the old habits, the old responses to emotions that no longer serve you.

From this moment onward you get to explore your feelings, thoughts and actions to learn from them rather than push them down, ignore them or project them onto another. These are your messengers. I remember an old Kabbalah teacher of mine many years ago who once asked, "if you don't open up your mail to read the letters how are you able to understand the message?"

Being self responsible means opening up your own mail and reading the letters that your body, mind and emotions are sending you. Relating in such a way invites in more intimacy, more creativity, more space to grow. This is how you will deal with your emotional body going forward.

Today I invite you to make that commitment to yourself. I would suggest writing down a few statements or a paragraph and placing it on your mirror to read every morning upon waking. This is the gift of presence you are here now to offer to yourself because you are worth it!

This space I am speaking of is space to rededicate yourself to cultivating the relationship with yourself in a way you would want a lover to be with you, with what excites you, with paying attention to every small component of your day to stay awake and be present to the smallest of gifts.

Now that you are beginning to relax into your new clean inner house, in the comfort of tidier rooms, you have more awareness around you that is from the past. You are now clear to be in the present moment. Your reactions of the past are beginning to shift.

# Self Sourcing and the Relationship with Yourself

Today I sit in ceremony in deep devotion to myself, to my body, heart, soul, blood and bones. The stillness calls me to awaken to a new sense of enthusiasm, creativity and pure joy. And so I make a personal promise to live intimately connected to myself.

Dear Self: to you I offer an apology for the ways I may have stumbled, lost my path at times. I am sorry for the moments I may have not listened, pushed myself harder than was in the highest good. For no matter what, you always take care of me, unconditionally. For this I am humbly grateful.

Today I make an offering. I place upon the earth all which has bound me, all that I have allowed to keep me captive and held down. I offer that which no longer serves the full richness of my creative energy to be birthed into full expression in the world.

Take this offering, Mama Earth, into your rich soils, to be recycled anew. So the fresh fertilizer nourishes new growth, new gardens and forests to flourish.

I promise to take care of my body, to be in deep listening. I am in divine partnership with this body-temple, heart , soul, body and mind. I promise to listen, love, pause, rest, slow down, play, laugh and touch.

Weaving together the priestess, lover, mother, child, wild woman, the dark and light, I surrender to the highest of paths for this being. Today I let go of fight, struggle, force, and allow my inner warrior to return to peace and presence in this partnership.

I bow in deep reverence to living in radical intimacy with all that lives and grows within me and around me. I return in allowing the ever changing ways of nature to be of my path. To love more, to live more, to feel more, to be more.

So Be it, So it is AHO!

A relationship requires a certain level of commitment and obligation. When I say relationship, I'm not just considering romantic relationships with a partner or spouse, I'm considering all of the relationships possible in our lives; relationships with family, children, friends, co-workers. I'm also talking about everything and everyone that you engage with throughout your day, week and life. All of these relationships require a certain expenditure of energy during the life of the relationship, and that isn't a bad thing. Relationships give us the opportunity to be consumed with joy, love, and happiness. The expenditure each relationship requires varies depending on the circumstances, but there is always a little something that is taken from you and put into the relationship. You are outputting, taking action and using fuel to engage with all of these relationships and it is consuming. In order to remain alive and viable, a relationship requires a certain amount of energy to live, get nourished and to thrive.

A great analogy for a relationship is a plant. Plants need water, sunlight, nourishment and attention in order to grow. Like each relationship, each plant has different requirements. Some prefer a little water, others need more, and some might need just a little light, while others need constant exposure to sunshine. Managing all of these relationships can be overwhelming and consuming. For that reason, we need to pay attention to ourselves and make sure that we don't allow the fuel within us to burn low. Remember that all relationships stem from the relationship with the self. When you nourish your relationship with your self this will be fuel for your relationships with others. Commit to maintaining your relationship with you!

I want to acknowledge that there may be times to come (or

maybe the present day) where you feel taxed, and struggle to have the quality of time in relationship with yourself that you want. You may feel overwhelmed, running in circles and not sure where to go from here because in addition to your partner, lover or business relationships you feel to be loosing yourself. When you're feeling this, it is time to begin to say no to those external draws of energy, which means you are saying yes to yourself. This is the time to ask "Have I stepped away from self sourcing?" I want to share a very personal story about just this. If your relationship with your own body, mind and spirit is lost, how can you expect to have a fueling relationship in any other area of your life? You will go on surviving but never living.

*When Life Happens*

In the beginning of 2016 I began to piece all my work over the past two decades together to write this book. It was a dream of mine to give you the gems to create a new view of relating for the world. When I started writing I realized that I had two different messages that needed to be split up into two books. I found myself working on two book projects at the same time. In addition, I was focused as an entrepreneur to keep my business growing, mentoring my students, and going to various networking events, luncheons and group meetings as part of my relationship building. I was also in the midst of a radical relationship transition with my primary partner at the time. As you can imagine, life was full with relating! And I also had a dedicated Vipassana meditation practice which was between one to two hours a day, a daily yoga practice, and required time to recharge and replenish myself as part of my self care practice.

Sounds full? Yes. I have been so blessed with such a full life. In October 2016 I had levels of fatigue which were becoming debilitating. I had a brain fog and an emotional overload that was making it excessively stressful to keep all of my commitments and stay organized. Before too long it became clear that the way it was going was impossible to continue. At that time I received help from a colleague to go see an Integrative Medicine specialist. It was at that time, after an abundance of tests that I was diagnosed with chronic limes, mold toxicity and mycotoxin overload. My bloodwork showed that my nervous system required me to slow down and go back to the basic and important relationship with myself—self sourcing.

You can imagine the feelings that arose when I received this diagnosis, the questions that bubbled up. What if all which I had worked for fell apart? What if I were unable to do what I was called to do on this planet? What if people saw me as broken, and what was going to happen through the big relationship change?

I sat in stillness at this point of my life and remembered what a dear colleague and friend once said to me: nothing is more important than the health of your body and mind. Without these you will be unable to do anything or share what you heart is called to share in the world.

I sat and it was clear at this phase of life nothing else mattered but me dropping into only that which fueled me. This had become a necessity for me to thrive!

I remember waking up some days with the questioning ringing in my head "What if I am dying?" Tears would flow down my cheek because I felt such an urgency to experience various lands, environments, people and wildlife as a means of gaining wisdom, and I worried I would never get the chance.

I felt I had so much more to experience and so much more to share.

I'm sharing this with you because every life contains some choices which are not easy. Our personal struggles and our life environment can not be compared to that of another. How we experience something is defined by our past and another person's past is different from your own.

I am grateful that I was born with discipline and tenacity. However, when this diagnosis hit me, it was the first time in my life I worried that it could all be over at any moment.

It affected my cognitive thinking. my sensitivity to chemicals skyrocketed. And yes, it certainly forced me to make many new choices. I had to quickly find a new home that was mold and chemical free, which meant having temporary homes for a month or two months at a time. My body did not have the stamina it used to have, so I was invited to reflect on what environments and activities added to my life and which took away.

I had to tone down a lot of the networking and business luncheons, and I began mentoring students part time. I began taking two or three weeks off at a time to be in places that had quieter, cleaner environments. A place to feel at peace in my body became essential.

Life is punctuated by moments and circumstances that call us to reflect on the quality of our relationships, and the quality of the relationship with our own self. If something is out of alignment in your relationship with yourself, life may in some way redirect you as it had redirected me.

The question still remains, what quality of life and relating will you choose. Let go of the victim story or the belief that it is to hard to change. Yes, sometimes it feels fucking hard. You are perfectly human and are going to feel a lot I would hope.

The difference is getting sucked into the victim abyss or being able to witness and acknowledge the victim story and continue to be proactive.

I remembering days where I felt sadness, I felt scared, lonely, angry, frustrated, confused, and it was my personal discipline to cultivating my own emotional intelligence, that provided me with the means to be proactive in my decisions, even in the edgier moments. I am able to let go of the victim story, and choose a different story, one where I have a deep, committed and healthy relationship with myself.

I know now that my relationship with my body, mind and spirit require simplicity, quiet, ease, and clean air to thrive. I also know this too will change. This is a season, and now I get to continue to share my work and care for myself in ways that add life rather than diminish life. You too, get to pause, take a breath and tap into your inner courage, and discover what your relationship with yourself truly needs.

In the next section, I have outlined some Do's and Don't's that will help you commit to keeping the relationship with yourself alive, healthy and vibrant, even as it evolves.

*Do's and Don't's*

**Do:**

**Do get still, relax and shut of** — It is important to set aside some time every day just for you. No phones, no computers and no one else. Whether it is a time for mediation, writing in a journal or just sitting quietly, this time is critical for recharging your batteries.

**Do listen to your body** — Your body is the most important barometer of how you are feeling and what you need. So start listening to it. When you are tired, rest. When you are hungry, eat. We need to listen to both the physical and emotional messages that our bodies send us. How are we feeling? What do we need? Breathing is one of the best techniques for listening to our bodies. Is your breath short and constricted? Are we feeling our breath into each cell of our bodies? Once you become aware of your breath, you can use it as a tool for measuring, sensing, locating and defining each of your experiences. By listening to these messages your body is sending and acting on them, we are making ourselves and our relationships more vibrant and fulfilling.

**Do know what things and experiences you are a no to and which ones you are a yes to** — As individuals, each person has different needs, wants and desires. Often it is taught that other people's needs are more important than our own. Or that because your partner or friend like certain activities or to be touched a certain way, that you are expected to like and even do the same. Doing things out of expectations or guilt will only create separation at some level. When in a relationship, often there is an eagerness to please the other party and a tendency to allow your own needs to take less importance.

For example, let's say that in order to be ready for the day, you start getting prepared for bed at 9:00 pm. You have a friend who likes to call you at this time, and, not wanting to hurt your friend, you take the call even though you know it will affect your rest. When you hear that phone ring, you may notice judgments and feelings of agitation and frustration. Plus, you'll wake up tired, unable to be as productive as you would like to be in your day. The build up of tiredness, the emotions and judgments, saying yes when you're really a no is a recipe for disaster in any relationship.

As soon as this is realized the process of understanding, expressing needs and creating a win/win situation can begin.

By saying no with compassion and a willingness to create a new call time that meets both party's needs, you build a sense of intimacy and connection that would not otherwise have been there.

Do stand by your core values — We all have values that are important to us. Trust, honesty and loyalty are just a few that come to mind for me. These values are what make us unique individuals. If your relationships are causing you to move away from these values or your relationship partner doesn't treasure these values, it may be time to re-evaluate the relationship. Reflect and get honest with yourself about which values you need to have 100% met in your relationship and which values you feel good with 50% or less of a match. When you move from a place of integrity, your relationships align to meet you there, or they will transition to a fit that better serves the values of everyone involved.

**Do take a day off** — Remember to take a whole day off, just for you. No phones, no appointments, no online updates. Unplug from the everyday and take the time to really see the world you are living in. Look at the trees, people and animals that are a part of your neighborhood. Take a walk through the park. Focus on what is going on around you. Many times we miss out on things that are happening right in front of us because we are too busy with other distractions.

**Don't:**

**Don't forget to use your ears and heart** — Deep Listening is an essential part of any relationship. Others want to be heard, understood and to know that their thoughts and opinions matter. So instead of thinking about the next thing you are going to say, look at the speaker intently and let them know that you are listening to what they are saying. Your body language can do a lot of this for you. Nodding and leaning in are signs that you are engaged in the conversation and are ready to hear more.

**Don't make their problem your problem** — Whether a problem is an ongoing one that was brought into the relationship or one that came about after the relationship began, don't make someone else's problem your problem. Just because you are in a relationship, it doesn't mean that you should share problems. It is important to let them know that you understand the issue they are dealing with and that you are there for them, but this is their battle.

**Don't lose yourself** — Especially in new relationships, we have a tendency to put the interests of the other party ahead of our own. We go to their favorite places, do their favorite activities and our likes and interests take second place. It is important to take turns doing activities. Make sure you are doing things that you like as well so that your interests don't get lost and their interests don't replace your own.

**Don't forget to tend and nurture** — Each relationship needs attention. Without attention, the relationship will wither and die. Remember our plant analogy? Relationships need to be watered and fed instead of left to fend for themselves. It takes presence and your attention to create and maintain a positive healthy relationship.

**Don't be afraid to walk away** — Even with our best intentions, there are relationships that either run their course or become too consuming in certain ways to continue. You may notice they drain you more than fuel you and your life-purpose. When this happens, it is okay to walk away from the way the relationship is now and allow it to come into what I call "Right Relationship." The most important person in your life is you. If a relationship is harming the relationship that you have with yourself, it is in your best interest to put your needs first, feeling into what you are needing and feeling. This will give you the capacity to make an empowered choice to walk away from the relationship if needed.

### *Self Sourcing is Fuel for All Your Relationships*

I want to share one of the tools my beloved and I have used to cultivate more juice and passion, and widen the depths of our love for one another. We have placed space and solo time on the top of our list for ways to deepen our bond.

Every year, I choose a five to six week solo journey on the road, usually in Canada (my favorite place). It gives me time to direct all my energy back to my center where life calls me deeper into me. Each day flows with meditation, Deep Listening, walks through the forest, and yoga. It is where I become so empty. I let the stress of doing evaporate. I draw my energy back to my center, into myself. I harness all that sweet juicy goodness right here into myself, my body and my spirit.

As I remember back to our Skype dates my beloved and I have had while I was on the road, I remember that passion birthed from my own center. I love how even when we are apart, we connect like we are sitting right next to each other. I love how my eyes see through my heart by going into this deep inner space for extended periods of time. I have built a new sensitivity to feel more of us because I am feeling more of myself.

The outcome of turning back to yourself and what fuels your own passion is that it only inspires more turn-on when it is time for your reunion with your loved ones and partner! After my space and solo time, I am able to share so much more of myself with my beloved as well as at work and play with colleagues and friends. This is due to taking responsibility to come into the relationship with my inner pilot light already burning bright.

Even in the most brilliant, juiciest, passionate partnerships, space and solo time are essential nutrients in order to grow the garden of your relationship. Feeding the self relationship allows relationships with others to blossom.

# Entering a Relationship Self Sourced

Whether it is a romantic relationship, marriage, friendship or a colleague. How we relate can uplift, empower and open us up more to our individual truth, love and connection. It can also support our partner's or friend's truth even as they are different from our own.

A glitch in relationships of any kind that often takes place is when you enter into the relationship thinking the other person (or the relationship itself) is there to fill your void, your needs, your wants. When that happens, the dynamic becomes you versus the relationship as a whole.

A part of you, that wounded part, may say "I do desire someone to fill my needs, someone to be responsible for my worthiness and security." Remember that you are reacting from a conditioned state. The little girl or little boy that still lives inside you is acting out from that place when they did not get the love they so deserved, or the attention from a parent, or inclusion in a group of peers. You must be aware when when these open wounds get triggered, that it is your wounded parts trying to claim what they missed or lost out on in the past.

I enjoy people-watching. One day I was observing adult relationships in the world and I noticed how humans adults are children in big bodies choosing relationships with mommy and daddy. Grown adults are still grasping to have the person of their attention fill all their needs. You can imagine, and you may have experienced, how tiring and, over time, unfulfilling this is. Like a dog chasing its own tail, endless cycles.

However, on some level this is not giving your what your heart and spirit yearn for. Love and connection, real connection, cannot be placed in such a rigid small safe box. This box will suffocate the life out of what you are seeking. Love is not safe!

Real Love is Free. We enter in an experience of relationship out of a choice to share our own full cup of love not out of a need to have someone else fill our cup, or out of obligation to fill the cup of another.

On the superficial level where do you only think of yourself, place these responsibilities on others and literally give away your own personal power? Where have you had felt a void and told yourself that your partner or business project was going to fill that void?

By doing so, you are actually moving farther away from love, you move farther away from your creative power, you are moving farther away from what you are seeking and you are suffocating the relationship at hand. Personally or professionally.

Focusing only on yourself in a relationship can look, on the surface, like the exact opposite. You were taught to give, give, give; and most give from a place of fear rather than from a place that truly aligns with their hearts. If you are emptying your cup so much eventually there won't be anything else to give. This is where attachment and excessive neediness forms. Naturally you will unconsciously grasp at what and who is closest to fill your cup: they become the bottomless cup that eventually breaks. Though your actions may look like you're focusing on your partner, the focus on your own fear means you are not caring for the relationship body.

*Wounded Relating Red Flags*

Here are some signs, some red flags that you are entering the danger cycle of it's-all-about-me.
- You expect your partner to want to do everything with you.

- Your partner does something you don't agree with and you blame them for how you feel.
- You feel you can't exist without the other person or a certain job, or project.
- You require validation from these people, boss or romantic partner, to be happy.
- The other person or people must behave in a certain way for your happiness.
- You are over-giving, or giving from an empty place, and forgetting to care for yourself.
- You blame others for how you feel.
- You are stuck in endless stories which make you the victim.

# Know Yourself to Know Another

This last section may seem like a bit of a paradox. Afterall, I have been sending the message that your relationship with others always stems from the relationship you have with yourself, and we have spent a whole half of this book focusing on improving your self relationship, only to end with a warning not to focus only on yourself in your other relationships!

But there is no paradox. All the effort we have expended on improving the relationship you have with yourself has been making space for you to have good healthy, vibrant relationships with others. In fact, all that space we have made for you own self relationship means you can take your focus off yourself in a relationship with others, and put it where it will bring the greatest amount of good in the world.

Also, the empathy and compassion you have developed for your own self can now be extended to others. Remember, you are the source of your own joy, you are the spirit and vibrancy that thrives at your center. And by having a good self relationship you can show up to your relationships with others with your cup full of that joy and vibrancy, ready to share in the joy and vibrancy that others bring to you.

# Part Two

# Relating to Others

# Being Authentically You in a Relationship

A common basic human need is to feel special. We all get that. Some ways which inspire us to feel special are when we feel treasured and adored in a relationship, to receive attention from a close friend, to receive an achievement award for something you did in business. Even though it is nice to receive attention and appreciation it is important that you remember how special you are just for being alive. Yes, you are a unique, amazing human being. It can be one of the biggest turn-on's for others as well when they see you owning your unique and authentic self. You will also begin to attract people who uplift and celebrate your authentic way of being; and those who don't, well, they will move on.

Let's acknowledge it can feel scary (this would be a great moment to allow in a deep belly breath) to be who you are rather than who you think someone wants you to be. "If I am different from the herd, I will loose friends, family, or possibly a job I had worked so hard for!" But the truth is you stand to lose so much more if you are not your authentic self.

Our partners are not where our fuel comes from, it is not where our joy comes from! We may share joy and happiness uniquely in a relationship, but that joy is already full inside of us.

Think back to what may have seemed a lifetime ago in the first part of this book. You were like a world class explorer diving deep into the inner caverns, caves and vast jungles of your inner-self. You did some intense landscaping, turning over forgotten stones, pulling up the old weeds, beginning to understand more about your actions, reactions and choices. By doing so, by committing to this profound relationship with your own body, mind and spirit you discovered the wellspring of your own happiness, and it is inside of you.

The work you did in part one was profound. It is also powerful. Lean on that work because in doing it, you have created much more capacity to show up in the fullness of who you are in your relationships. You are ready to shine your wisdom, your unique gifts, your brilliance, your power, and your charisma.

In the world where we have partners, love relationships, business relationships, friendships, and so many more relationships, establishing a unique bond with someone may seem a challenge. And we have all experienced some kind of relationship that felt absolutely flat, like there is just no connection. This is where showing up in your authentic self matters. It is essential that we realize our heart's unique connection with each person individually, and we cannot achieve that while trying to be someone else, someone generic.

*Reconnecting with Your Authenticity*

What happens when you start to feel like you might not be as authentic in a relationship as you might be, when your "I" starts to be subsumed by "we?" Well, part one of this book, The Relationship with One's Self, is full of all the work and practices that will guide and help you to be in touch with who you are at the core. But I have put the two most important ideas here to help keep you on track when you don't have time to go back and review.

**You must be in touch with and aware of what you are experiencing and feeling in the present moment** — Make sure you are keeping up with your daily breathing practice and other awareness practices.

**Are you remembering to self-source or have you or your partner got caught up in the dependency cycle?** — To self-source is to remember what fuels you outside of your partner and their choices. It goes back to joy being a choice. When we have fallen off the self-sourcing train is usually when you or your partner or even a friend will start to make you feel guilty for not choosing to do certain things with them when they want you to; you or they might become jealous when making other choices. During this stage a lot gets taken personally instead of honoring that what each other wants may be quite different, and that is okay.

You can see that the kernel of both of these ideas is that you must be your own authentic and responsible self.

# Boundaries

There is no doubt that when you're in a relationship with someone, their happiness becomes important to you. Listen in, I want to share these two sentiments on the happiness of a another: "I have to fulfill my partner's or friend's needs because it is expected of me," versus "I have everything, I am full and my partner's, friends' and colleagues' needs and values are so in alignment that I am overjoyed for them—happy to see their needs being met." Both sentiments have their partner's joy at the center of concern (and yes, some needs may be met by you out of a shared desire, not out of expectation or force), however one of those sentiments may suffocate the relationship, while the other will uplift the relationship and those involved.

Are you ready to become a master of your boundaries? This means you become a master at creating and attracting those ideal relationships personally and professionally. Boundaries are a powerful tool, a means to knowing yourself and knowing your partner as beautiful individuals coming together to share yourselves in a relationship.

Have you been raised to think that everyone else's needs are more important than yours? Do you constantly give until you feel exhausted. How about settling because someone else told you this was all you were worth? Do you find yourself constantly nagging at others to get what you what? Are you pushing other people so much they constantly feel they need to put up walls and be firm in their dialog with you? Do you feel unfulfilled, resentful, or even unsafe to be intimate or open with certain people?

These are some of the actions and responses that take place when you have over-stepped your own boundaries, allowed others to push beyond your boundaries or have no idea what it even means to have a boundary.

I have heard many ask, "aren't boundaries limiting?" My response is that it is more limiting to have no boundaries. Setting boundaries is an act of love towards yourself and another. They are guidelines in our human reality which take into account one's physical, emotional and psychological states in order to create situations that really nourish and provide room for more connection. Boundaries allow another to know you in this present moment; they allows you to know another.

Do you ever get that creeping feeling that you're being manipulated somehow? Being manipulated is quite common and it's not always that bad word we may think it to be. Manipulation can be as simple as a friend wanting to convince you that something is good for you, even if you really don't want it. Or has a lover pushed you into doing something with them when you really wanted to do something else in that moment? Those are examples of small manipulations. Later on, you probably noticed feeling an undertone of resentment for doing what someone else wanted instead of what was true for you. This is an example where boundaries and self-responsible communication would have been an asset (more on communication in an upcoming chapter).

I mentioned boundaries and borders earlier in the book. The difference between them is that boundaries changes when your state changes. You may have a certain boundary which assist you in feeling safe or which provides certain self care, you may find some time later that it does not serve you anymore and you feel clear to shift this boundary.

A border is what one puts up when they had no boundary in the first place. Borders are like brick walls that get slammed up out of a reaction, often when one feels unsafe, when one feels emotionally, physically or psychologically pushed. Borders are harder to move due to the emotional state which created them. They often break apart partnerships, disrupt relationships and break up business collaborations as well.

When you are unaware of your own boundaries you won't be great at detecting and respecting someone else's boundaries. That could leave others feeling unsafe, guarded, and what happens is that all parties involved begin to create borders. In order to set your boundaries it will take self inquiry, compassionate communication skills, and learning the art of delivering at the perfect time. Let's look at self-inquiry.

*Feel and Understand your Feelings*

Have we spoken about the importance of understanding and feeling your feelings? This is a skill set which is required in order to set clear boundaries. By now you have developed a considerable set of tools for self inquiry while you were consciously deepening your relationship with yourself. Reflect upon that self inquiry and I am sure you will recall situations where you felt overwhelmed, unsafe in the presence of another. Did you ever feel exhausted after an event and realized it really didn't match what you needed in the moment?

When you say yes to something that doesn't really fuel, or match your authentic yes, you may think you are creating connection. But where is the connection if, underneath it all, you are contracted, counting the minutes for something to be over, and wishing you were elsewhere? After the fact, you are tired and feeling disconnected, and in time, resentment builds. You are on a route to loosing yourself in any relationship that functions that way. This is common. It can even happen in business where the people working together become so enmeshed that they no long know what their own truth is. They stop expressing their true deep passions and desires. Creativity becomes stagnant.

By choosing to take the time, giving yourself permission to really feel what your entire body and psyche need in that moment before jumping into a yes, you are choosing to stay connected to who you are as a sovereign empowered being. Without this, it is impossible for another to get to really know you.

### *Where Have You Ignored Your Boundaries*

A good way to improve your boundary setting skills is to look at the times and places where you have ignored your boundaries. Begin with reflecting and make a list of situations where someone has asked too much of you, and you gave it to them. It might be as common as taking calls after a certain hour and waking up exhausted the next day, going out to a party or event because your felt it was expected of you but you really wanted to stay in and take a bath or write in your journal. Do you have clients that show up time and time again without their preparation work completed, or arrive late or cancel continuously? These are example of boundaries being crossed.

In the earlier section on unwinding I shared with you my growing need to unwind and slow down because I had not been setting my boundaries. At the time I was in the business of networking. My desire was to meet and mingle to find the right business relationships. I went out continually to network and come home feeling exhausted and lacking in creativity. Along the way I had stopped following what my body, mind and heart were really being called to do. I would get emails asking if I was attending this event or that event and I lost touch with my natural inner guidance for a bit. When I finally stepped back, unwound, and got real with my feelings, it became clear that the cause of my depressed energy and creativity was all the overcommitments. Once I knew what was creating this state, and how this state really felt in my body, I was able to be super clear on my boundaries and needs.

It helped to adjust how much I was outputting. My personal boundary of no more than one three-hour luncheon once a month aligned with my needs. And every so often, when I was invited to speak or co-lead a circle, I would attend one of the networking groups, but otherwise I chose other avenues that fueled my creative passion. Sure enough creativity was in abundance again. Doing what I loved to do, feeling fulfilled in my business and being back in my pleasure rocked! Seeing pleasure is a part of my business.

Now it's your turn. Go back to those situations you listed, and how you felt during them. Make a list of what you would need to feel more energy, fuel, and harmony in this situation. Does the sitution need to end completely, do you need to adjust the parameters of the situation or how you and another person engage? Do you need to shut your phone off earlier, make clearer business time lines or set new boundaries on how often you help a friend that may always be in need of your help?

### Sexual Boundaries

Your sexual boundaries are just as important as any other. Do you and your partner assume everything in the bedroom is a yes simply because you are dating? Have you ever been asked "what are you boundaries?" and you didn't know what to say, so, feeling a little embarrassed, you just mumbled something like "I don't have any boundaries... I am a pretty open person."? Well guess what, I bet I would be able to find one or two sexual boundaries of yours if I dug deep enough. So I am going to invite you to explore this for yourself.

Repeat the same process that you went through above. Reflect, perhaps make a list of moments or experiences from your sexual history where you didn't feel so good, but you just went along with it because you were in the moment or you were trying to please someone. Once it is clear how these experiences felt in your body and what your response to them was, make a list of what you were needing in each one of those moments, what you would have liked instead. What would have felt more fulfilling for you?

These needs might be how you're touched, when you're touched, where you're touched. It could pertain to which situations or environments you choose to be in and where you feel safe.

When it comes to sex, so much of what we understand about our partner's wants and needs is sometimes left up to guesswork and assumption. Good sex comes with good communication! And don't go thinking that you know your partner's immediate needs just because you've been with them for a long time; this extends to those of you in long term relationships too. Your state changes depending on your energy levels and emotions. This means your sexual boundaries change, and so do those of your partners.

Working with your partner to understand each other's boundaries is when the true magic of setting boundaries becomes clear. By inquiring to your partners desires, needs and boundaries in the present moment you open an invitation to know each other at a new immediate level. You become more authentic with each other, and that in turn opens up the experience to more pleasure because no one feels like they have to pretend. The pressure is off.

## Setting Boundaries

Before you can set a boundary, you have to be clear on what you are a yes to, what you are a no to. Listen to your body, it is where your true intelligence lives. It will know. Everything you have read and experienced in this book until this point are keys to being more grounded, centered and clear within yourself. You will find that your daily practice with breathwork, self-inquiry and awareness makes exploring your boundaries easier.

Delivering your message is not always easy. We will be exploring communication in depth in a coming chapter, and you will want to use all those compassionate communication skills and practices when you communicate your boundaries to others. For now, I will give you a couple of basic ideas that are central to boundary communication.

Take care of yourself. I used this analogy before: remember to put your oxygen mask on first. You will not be able to help another understand your boundaries or explore and disclose their own if you are not in a good enough state. Take some self time, go into an experience which nourishes you. Maybe a walk in the forest, nature time, the beach, gym or yoga class.

If someone expresses anger or upset about your boundary, invite in a self-responsible form of communication. Can they express and own their feelings? If they are projecting and blaming or shaming you, this would be a perfect time to set another boundary. Call a red flag—pause the conversation and take space. "I am sorry but I am unable to hear what you are needing right now due to the strong language or emotional upset. When you are ready to communicate in a clearer, calmer manor, I would be happy to return to our conversation. Until that time I am going to pause here and take my space." Make sure to set a time that feels good for all of you to revisit the topic.

Remember it's all practice, we all trip up from time to time. I invite you to let go of perfection and remember you must take a first step to be closer to the quality of relating you desire.

# Moving Beyond Right — The Art of Compassion

In seeking to deepen understanding with other people, it is beneficial to remember that you are responsible for yourself. The flip side of that coin means you have no real control over another person. And would you really, deep down inside, want to control someone you care about? When you're dealing with another keeping in mind that you don't have any real control over them, and keeping in mind what your desired outcome is, empowers your ability to make clearer decisions. This opens you up to collaboration and cooperation in getting everyone's needs met.

This may not be easy when you are feeling angry, disrespected and not getting the care and love you desire. Remember we all want love and connection, even those who are screaming at you to be heard. All that groundwork that you did in the first part of this book—your daily breathwork practices and starting to understand your emotional upsets and triggers—will assist you.

Most people have a limited capacity when they feel overwhelmed or attacked. When people feel the energy of blame coming at them along with all the chaos and drama that it brings, they shut down, they run away. Arguing and fighting often come from a fear of not being heard. Remember, upset equates to unmet needs. Emotions are messengers about what one is needing. If we take the time to listen to those messengers we can deepen understanding, increase compassion and get away from right and wrong.

This is a hard shift to make, but it is absolutely fundamental.

## *Pairbonds are Triads*

Before I get into the tools for deepening your understanding, I want to get you to acknowledge an often overlooked third entity in any relationship between two people: the relationship itself. A relationship between two people is an entity all on its own, as is the relationship that you have with yourself and the relationship your partner has with themselves. So truly within a pair bond, there are three separate relationships happening at once. This is an idea I first came across in Adyashanti's audio course, The One of Us.

It has always made sense to me that the relationship we co-create with another over time becomes a life of its own. We weave together multiple individual self-relationships into one larger relationship. Everything you are, your life-force, your essence, your atoms, molecules, breath, values, beliefs, emotions are being entwined with all of those unique aspects of another to create something bigger. All three of these entities have their own individual needs. Sometimes what is in the highest good for the individual is not the same for the relationship. All three are in constant flux.

When you experience a relationship in such a way your involvement with it becomes more about filling it with pure love instead of just seeing what you can get from it. You and your partner are not earning love from each other but rather love is where everything is birthed from. In this form of relating all involved are not dependent on the other for approval or love but you are all fueled by love.

In this stage relationship begins to take on a form that serves a higher purpose. When you as individuals in the relationship become so in-tune and come together with a shared higher purpose your needs begin to align, they become similar.

The other thing to remember in such a way of relating

is you are looking at what really serves, serves you and your partner and your relationship. You lose the focus on emotional wants in the moment or what makes you comfortable. This is where relationships becomes a spiritual practice.

With that in mind, let's do an exercise to jump into deeper understanding.

### *Journaling Beyond Judgment*

The exercise below is a step by step journaling process to move beyond judgment and into understanding. Curiosity will be your ally here. You can do this on your own or you can do this together with your partner, friend or colleague. If you do this with another, I highly suggest you do the entire process quietly on paper before you share. You will want to go slowly. Feel the feelings inside your physical body and write them down.

1. Acknowledge what you or another is feeling. Be curious, get still, take some breathes. This may take a moment or two. Identify the feelings simply: I am feeling _____. Sad, angry, resentful, scared, frustrated, mad, rage etc…

2. Imagine you were the other person or people involved. Really put yourself in their shoes. What might they be feeling? Write it down.

3. Identify what you are needing based on what you're feeling. Again, keep it simple. It is often the case that emotional want triggers us to complicate it. What am I needing? I'm needing to take space and reflect; I'm needing to be heard; I'm needing to be included; I'm needing reassurance; I'm needing connection…

4. Imagine you are the other person or people. Put yourself in their shoes. What might they be needing based on

their feelings? Write it down. And remember to allow the time to pause and really feel here.

5.   Now go deeper into the needs you wrote above. If you needed to take space and reflect, outline what would that look like? If you needed to be included, what might that look like? Write out a tangible description.

After you have gone through steps one to five sit quietly, reflect on the feelings you now have about understanding yourself and someone else better.

Coming to a better understanding of your feelings and needs, and someone else's feelings and needs, erodes the stories of blaming, judging and condemning. Your curiosity helped open this door. After doing this exercise, you will typically find that when you do go into a conversation with the person concerned, your heart is more open to listening and it organically creates a new environment for productive connection. From this place, so much more is possible.

## When They Don't Have the Desire or Ability to Understand You

I was in a situation recently where no matter how clearly, compassionately and willingly I communicated, the other person was not in a place to hear me. Whatever I did to discover what they needed, or to express mindfully what was alive in me, it was met with a brick wall. Don't expect everyone in your life to have a skill of deep presence or a desire to deconstruct your story to find out your feelings and needs. Ultimately it is not their job, though it is certainly a bonus in the relating department.

In these moments, it is important to remember the desired outcome: you are aiming for deeper connection and love. The more empowered you are, the more responsible you can be, creating more win/wins in your life for you to experience and share with others. Don't be upset when others aren't able to meet you in this approach.

I remember implementing breathing in my belly, remembering that they too had an emotional history, they had specific needs that were not being met in that moment. I could imagine what they were feeling, and what they wanted. You see, staying open and curious is essential for your peace. I acknowledge I felt frustration and certainly owned my degree of tiredness. I did the best I could by applying all the tools, making requests, as I stayed present with what I was feeling, it was clear, the importance of not wanting to convince this person of anything. Experiences like this may require self soothing afterward.

Stepping into activity that fueled myself up after this uncomfortable conversational run-in was a priority. Being proactive and setting a boundary around engagement with this person during my stay and knowing my bottom line were steps I took with awareness and mindfulness of what both of us were needing in this moment.

Remember, be mindful of taking things personally. It could have been so easy to do so. With so many different upbringings, cultures, emotional burdens and traumas, no two people are alike. I believe this would make for a dull world if we were all the same. Variation and our many different perspectives help us grow and evolve.

Don't take it personally when your in-laws criticize your cooking, when your colleague disagrees with your opinion, when your school mates don't agree with your fashion sense and tease you. Rather, share what you are feeling, share what would feel good to you. Share your view and move away from any defensive mode.I know it doesn't feel good to be on the other end of these responses. Understand that people make fun of or criticize what they don't understand, what they fear and what they were taught to criticize. The practices in this book are designed to shift these habits, change the fear into new found enthusiasm and curiosity. The intention is to know yourself and others to a new degree.

Empowered disagreements, on the other hand, are an opportunity to get curious and ask why the other person feels or thinks a certain way, to express the reasons for your choices not out of defense but as a way for you to express who you are. We will talk more about empowering language when we dig deeper into communication.

Be clear on your needs in the moment and express clear boundaries. Be Proactive. Create a plan for how you will create ease and fulfill your needs to the best of your ability with what you have in the moment. Do you see a plan to shift this over the next weeks or months?

I had a client named Andy. He was dedicated on his spiritual path and was learning so much about his relational values through his work in the Soulful Relating Program. However, his challenge was that he had a partner who did not have the same interest. He would go away and dive into learning all these new tools on communication, expansive relating and mindfulness, and yet when he arrived home she seemed uninterested. She had a busy life raising their children and preferred to spend her free time watching TV or reading fantasy novels. You can imagine the frustration that Andy experienced wanting to share his newfound joys and interests, or his disappointment that his partner didn't have the skills he was learning when they tried to sort out disagreements.

Andy felt unloved, that his partnered did not care about

him. This is a good example of a situation where one partner is not available for the kind of connection the other yearned for. What do you do when this happens? The most important thing is to realize that even though you are in a relationship you have individual needs and values, and that those needs change over time. Andy's perception that he was unloved was the story he was creating in his mind about the situation.

Over time Andy committed to his own inner work, disengaging his emotional story about being unloved and showing up more in his life with self confidence, presence, and the ability to communicate his boundaries with compassion and love even in the midst of a disagreement. He finally felt so comfortable with who he was that he found himself more honest about his feelings and needs and less scared of loosing someone.

When we show up in such a way it actually allows any relationship to blossom and evolve in an empowered way.

### *Don't Argue With Reality*

There is a wonderful sentiment expressed by Byron Katie that says if you argue with reality, you will always lose. The reality is that some people won't have the skill or desire to understand you. Here are a few tips that can keep you from arguing with that reality.

**Acknowledge the change in needs** — Everyone changes over time, as does their relationship to themselves and their relationships to others. It is important to recognize this evolution and acknowledge it. Show yourself compassion!

**Own your evaluation of the situation and get curious** — Being straight forward, asking about what the other likes or enjoys about their present situation or experiences makes a big difference. Let them know how you feel and what you might desire without demanding they fulfill it.

**Exercise your choice** — You are responsible to see that your needs are met and you have to make a choice about how to do that. Andy's choice was to continue to cultivate his skills, live his life and raise his family with his partner. He chose to accept their differences and even his disappointment, and in time he developed communities of friends who did have shared values and interests. His relationships with his partner met the needs of raising children together, and there was love there.

You choice in a similar situation may be different. When we are relating at home, work or play and it feels like you are exhausting yourself pushing a square peg into a round hole, this is where you might choose to walk in another direction. It is a choice versus a reaction.

When you are with someone who does not have the desire or ability to understand your opinion or needs, remember it is not their job to do so. It would feel good if they did, but remember it's not that someone is disagreeing with you that causes you pain, it is fighting against that reality of what is that creates suffering.

## Deep Listening

We have been developing a new set of awareness skills and applying them to our self relationships. Now we are extending those tools to our relationships with others. One of the skills we developed in the first part was Deep Listening. Deep Listening is a skill that helps you come to fully know your own self, your needs and desires. The methods of Deep Listening with yourself are personal and we looked at journaling, speaking honestly with friends and daily breathing practices as ways to do it.

Deep listening serves the need to be understood that we all have. Removing the fear of not being heard makes way for a new empowering kind of communication.

I will outline the steps for Deep Listening between two people, but first I want to go over some considerations. These considerations come back to putting your oxygen mask on first. If you're not able to engage in Deep Listening properly, you won't be helping if you try.

**Be self aware** — Be aware of your present state, physically, psychologically, emotionally and mentally. Do you have the energy and capacity to listen deeply to another in this moment?

**Be honest** — If you don't have the energy and presence, own it! If you have the capacity and you're willing to offer it to another person, create the structure for it.

**Set a time frame** — If now is not the time, set a time that would work better for everyone. Or if you are available on all levels to listen deeply, how long are you available? Or agree on a cue you will give when you are at capacity. I like to be safe and set a timer for 15 minutes and check in at that time to see how we are feeling.

**Practice compassion** — Before the deep share, ask questions, make requests, and be clear on your own needs. Deep Listening is a gift, if you are doing it out of a sense of obligation, it's no longer a gift.

Some things that may help open up the share are breathing together, sitting side by side or facing each other depending on the relationship. Don't rush, get grounded and then go...

*Steps to Deep Listening*

1. Check in and make sure you are in a place where you have the capacity, the energy, and bandwidth to really offer

the other person your undivided attention and presence. For example, "I can feel your excitement to share this, and you deserve my 100% presence in this conversation. However, I am noticing I am feeling rather exhausted and have so many things on my mind. How would you feel if I took some times to finish the projects I have on my plate and we sit and talk in two hours?" Share authentically. If you don't have the capacity, let them know that you understand the importance and that they deserve presence. Make sure to schedule, this shows their importance and value.

2. If you are available, move forward and make sure you are in a room that doesn't have distractions.

3. Tell your partner what you would like to share. Using empowered language, share from the I. For example, I feel excited, I feel sad, I noticed I felt jealous when this happened. Sharing from the I is taking ownership of your feelings rather than projecting your perspective story onto them.

4. Be sure you have understood the other person, and be sure they know it by saying or asking. Be mindful to resist mechanically repeating "I hear you." For example, "If I understood you correctly, You feel hurt when _____, and you desire to_____. Is this correct?"

5. Be sure you listen to all the other person has to say. This will prevent any emotions or unspoken words from lingering in the process which could create resentment and upset. You might ask, "Would you like to share more or elaborate on this so I may really understand what you are feeling or desiring?"

6. Tune in to your empathy. Put yourself in the other person's shoes as best you can. This really allows the

other person to know that even if you disagree that you are in this together as a team. As the other person shares and you are doing your best to know their experience, you can reflect the understanding back with statements like "If I were you I could imagine I would be feeling _____."

7. Once the sharing is complete, calmly repeat what you heard and understood. In this repetition you are acknowledging their personal truth and needs or requests. You do not need to agree in order to acknowledge, but it is important to do it. Acknowledgments soften the desire to defend or fight and opens the door to more of a win/win outcome. It helps people lean in for more. Acknowledge in a way that will reach their hearts and body. For example, "I can imagine how challenging this situation is for you," or "what you are asking is completely understandable and you deserve this."

After a Deep Listening session, you may want something from the other person. It's important to communicate this desire as a request and not as a demand. Demands have a tendency to be met with resistance. Requests are gifts with pretty bows on them, they are an opportunity to share truly what it is you're needing or wanting in this moment. If you are making a request, I suggest you start with something simple and present. If you're working with a loved one, you might ask to share a hug, or for a loving gesture. If with a business colleague or associate, your request may be to communicate differently, or to receive a small gesture that would make the project easier and more productive. Now you have created a platform that will begin to create greater trust and safety.

# Communication

We want our feelings to be understood, and our needs to be met. The way to get what we want is to get clear and direct in our communication. Don't be afraid to get inquisitive and ask! Talk about things that challenge you. I know from working with many people over the years, as well as from my own life path, that full transparency eliminates so many unnecessary misunderstandings and drama in relationships. It prevents unnecessary emotional pain without avoiding emotional experiences.

Transparent and empowered communication is reassuring because it offers support and safety. You have already begun to build those good communication skills. We have looked at Deep Listening, setting boundaries and increasing your self-awareness. All of those skills are communication skills. And we will fold them into a larger set of skills in this chapter.

Living a practice of Deep Listening, being responsible for your feelings and transparent in sharing them, being inquisitive and asking questions, co-creates a relationship that serves the needs of all and creates a deep level of intimacy and connection. This intimate connection, born from such transparency, is the key for sustainability in a relationship.

## Sources of Trouble in Communication

There is a lot that stands in the way of good communication. Many of us have been conditioned to hold things in, or to explode and project blame and shame on others when we are upset. We hold back our communication out of fear or hurt. We don't ask for what we need because we were told that it wasn't okay. This creates an explosion of emotions, resentment, and separation.

Have you ever had one of those moment where you felt

something, maybe your emotions were a bit triggered and when you went to speak your words were jumbled and the person you were speaking to seemed to not hear anything you said? Did you notice the person you were speaking to began to get tense as well? In your mind you may not be aware of why this is all happening. Neither one of you is hearing the other, both feeling attacked. This can happen because we use violent language and constructions when we try to communicate difficult things. Violent communication and being afraid to ask for what we want are destructive forces in relationships. Fortunately, there are good tools to overcome those destructive forces, and we will look at transparency and empowering language as good remedies. But first, I want to look at a common element of relationships that can be surprisingly limiting: agreements.

### Agreements as a Cage or Key to Freedom

Each day we make some form of agreement, whether it is in business, organizing our personal financial budgets, preparing for marriage, or when lovers are in a dialog about their values. Agreements create a structure for relationships to be created in and grow, a scaffold of sorts.

Agreements can be funny things though. In our minds we make agreements in order to create a sense of safety and security for ourselves and the future. They reassure us of what to expect with regard to the direction a business deal or relationship is going. Agreements help us evaluate, "is it worth my investment?" But the shadow side is that many of our agreements are made out of old emotional fears.

We don't do this deliberately. Our story runs the show. A relationship with agreements that were created out of fear has more of a box structure than an open field with room to grow. The box is safe, but confining, there is no room for the relationship to breathe or grow. It is created from old, limiting emotional patterns of insecurity. Can another person ever truly provide us security? We hold on really tight to the illusion that perhaps they can. What usually happens is we end up disappointed.

Often when I am feeling I need an agreement, it is because some part of me feels unsafe. Instead of being fearful and avoiding, I enjoy diving into this with those I'm in relationship with. Thinking out loud is a way I am able to deconstruct a belief to see where the fear is coming from. I ask myself, "Why do I need this agreement? How will this agreement support me in moving through this old pattern?" Ultimately, when I have partners willing to process with, thinking out loud with a lover, friend or partner who is present and holding the space and willing to be a part of my process, supports me in realizing what is true for me right now.

Agreements that are made from your unexplored fears can become a trap. If you are unaware of your old programming, limiting emotional patterns and agreements, your relationships may seem like a locked cage where the key has been thrown away. A classic example is that we make an agreement with a partner out of fear of not wanting to lose them. The agreement starts to feel like it is cast in stone, never to be broken or rewritten. The box becomes tighter, no one is breathing. Perhaps the one of us who needed the agreement is not willing to do the work or make any changes. All the fear inside us is running the show.

It feels suffocating because it is very limiting. It has created a false sense of safety, not a real one. It is not empowering you or the relationship. But, what if you created agreements out of awareness, to use as a key to unlock the door to empowered relationships? What if you consciously utilized agreements to uncover your old emotional patterns, to get to know the feelings buried underneath? What if you made agreements that helped you discover your needs and helped you to commit to shifting your patterns?

When agreements are well understood and well set, they can be a means of creating a safer space together with your lover. They can help you move through fear, rather than allowing the fear to trap you both. With that awareness in the present moment, I can discuss and agree upon what I need and want with my partner, in order to move through something. It gives me the opportunity to go deeper into love, celebration and freedom within the relationship. The intention is to explore, expose and choose from present moment awareness and freedom, so that my relationships can breathe in a wide open space.

Imagine being free of the fears that cage you in. Imagine being able to have everything you ever wanted with ease. Imagine being able to consciously and confidently create an experience where you meet your lovers, friends and family members in a way that is free from the cage of the past. Imagine finding the key that unlocks the cage and sets you and your partners free. Now that is love!

That key is awareness and the courage and willingness to be free from the cage of old patterns of the past. Use this key to unlock, uncover and expose all the hidden patterns that will set you and your partners free to co-create empowered communication, love and relating.

Close your eyes and feel into the first moment you met your partner, lover, friend, business associate. For me, there is usually a deep feeling of love and connection, before any words are ever exchanged. It is a feeling of connection that goes beyond words. Then over time, old patterns may begin to rise up. But don't be concerned, because this can actually be a beautiful thing. It is an invitation to reveal and discover something within you. Working through your fear-based controls expands and empowers the relationships, in order for you to grow in love rather than fear.

## Conflict in Communication

Communication has the power to create connection and intimacy or disconnection, separation and conflict. Have you ever had a difficult conversation that ends in silence, both parties walking away angry and unheard, their bodies in contractions? There is a good chance the conversation turned out that way because the people involved were using violent communication.

This happens when we feel conflict in our mind and body and project it onto another, either blaming judging, pointing the finger or simply delivering a message in a way that the other feels attacked. The interesting thing is that most of the world communicates this way. It is conditioned into us. "You did that, I did this, he or she hurt me, how dare they," and on and on. A key to breaking away from violent communication is to remember that communication is not about being right or wrong, it is about deepening our understanding and creating win/win scenarios.

Any of these behaviors should stand out as red flags of discordant communication: blaming another for your feelings; shaming or condemning; stating that someone else's feelings aren't real or valid; yelling and shouting if it is being used to convince someone you are right.

Any communication that attacks and projects, that is not willing to take in the whole picture and see everyone's point of view, any communication where you are making someone else responsible for your feelings and situation is violent communication.

Here are some examples: How dare you do this to me? You are so stupid for acting that way! Why the hell would you do it like that? There is no need to cry or be upset.

The best way to guide others into compassionate communication—into curiosity, into understanding not judging—is to be a good example. Modeling compassionate communication is one of the best guides in inviting another to do the same. I believe it is important to avoid taking on an authoritative teacher role where another has not agreed as they may become defensive and feel they are doing something wrong or feel patronized. This is why you modeling such quality in your communication is a great way to inspire someone else. It also keeps you from falling into a repeating cycle of harmful communication.

Get curious about the other person, acknowledge them for their hardship or for what they did, and ask if you may share your own feelings around the matter. And if sharing your perspective, always ask first. That way the conversation becomes more of an invitation, and human nature is to open up and get on that curiosity train. We become more interested when we don't feel forced into something. Remember the common thread: to be loved and understood.

## Empowering Language

Using empowering language, along with other communication skill like Deep Listening, is the antidote to harmful communication. Empowering language is when you use wording and delivery to express yourself from the I perspective.

You own what you are feeling, needing and thinking. I feel this. I thought that. I would like this. It has you making requests instead of demands of another person. The overall tone is welcoming and inviting, even when you are setting boundaries and agreements, whether you are at home or work.

I remember this lovely client, Chris. He was a business man, and highly intelligent. As we built our professional relationship, Chris kept on reminding me what a valued customer he was. Because he was a returning customer, he regularly intimated that he should receive special rates and deals. Valuing him and appreciating his willingness and courage, we unpacked this in one of our sessions. He acknowledged that his message came from the old business mentality "I scratch your back, you scratch mine." There seemed to be a lot of undertone of expectation in it, as if he desired to prove something. In one of our mentoring sessions, as he dove deep into developing his communication skills, we explored and discovered that he had developed this pattern over his 50 plus years in the corporate "dog eat dog world," as he would say.

I invited him to see if there was another way to deliver his message by expressing his feelings more. I appreciated him not only as a client but as a human being and valued how devoted and disciplined he was to really apply everything he was learning. How could he be more vulnerable and turn this into a request? Often we naturally give out of appreciation, it is a joy to do so. Here we turn obligation into a huge desire to share.

Chris's eyes perked up and he got it. He expressed that really he wanted to share how much he was receiving from the Soulful Relating Program. Chris was able to re-frame his desire to work more closely with the Soulful Relating Institute by asking "do you offer any special VIP rates, or special options to have you on a retainer?" Getting curious and expressing his feelings was the key. Chris uncovered that when he had felt taken advantage of in business, his sense that he deserved more turned into an unattractive expectation that potentially could push people away.

Using empowering language does a better job of communicating because it lets others know not just what we want, but what we are experiencing too. It helps the listener open up to new ideas and helps them understand you better. It helps them feel compassion for your experience, even in the midst of a disagreement.

## Transparency / Communicating Your Authentic Self

When you hide, you create a prison that blocks true intimacy and limits your voice in the world. Transparency sets you free.

Many of us have been taught to hide our feelings, to not let others see them because it is inappropriate to actually speak truthfully about how we feel, to be vulnerable. We are told it could make other people uncomfortable. Yet, when we start hiding the present moment truth, we begin to create distance and walls. We unknowingly create separation and a false sense of being with another. Unconsciously, we start to create disease within our bodies and our relationships. Years later we are resentful and angry. We feel like we don't know who we, our partners or our friends are anymore. We wonder who this stranger that we are living with and also staring back at us in the mirror.

The art of transparency is about becoming vulnerable and willing to communicate at a deep intimate heart to heart level. I call it "the art of radical intimacy" because there is an art to being "real", vulnerable, exposed to being seen fully, while also being self responsible in how we express ourselves to others. It can be a tricky balance to be so transparent while feeling difficult, uncomfortable emotions that we may not know how to navigate. Vulnerability is sexy! Own it!

Let's look at an example. How often do you feel jealousy? Most of us, at one time or another, have felt jealous. Most likely, we were told jealousy was bad and wrong. It wasn't okay or safe to feel it, let alone communicate it to others. We were taught it wasn't safe or acceptable to let others know how we really feel. And yet, we still felt the uncomfortable feelings of jealousy anyway.

Not knowing it, we held our breath, trying to stop feeling jealous. Then we probably became moody and uncomfortable around others, pulling away and acting weird because they became triggers for those feelings in us. We pretended it wasn't there and suppressed it and moved on. By doing so, we created a disconnection within ourselves, ignoring and judging our feelings which leads to a disconnection from others over time. Our stories are suffocating.

Fast forward to the present day; what if you were to feel what you have come to know as jealousy? Now you have some tools you could use. You could pause and take a moment to get clear on what you are feeling instead of letting the Manic Mind take over and distract you with the story it is creating about those feelings. It could be as simple as acknowledging to yourself, "Okay, I'm feeling jealous right now." Notice what that jealousy feels like in your body. Do you have tightness in your chest? Perhaps you feel a bit tense in your belly.

Ask yourself "What am I scared of?" Your answer might be "I'm scared I'm not special", or "I'm worried someone is taking my place?" That's great because your feelings of jealousy are helping you get clear. As you get to know your feelings more, you learn more about the Manic Mind's past stories that keep you trigger happy.

When we go through an experience in which feelings are triggered but we push them down, those unspoken thoughts and feelings start to add up, which creates more separation and less connection to ourselves and our loved ones. Becoming more emotionally aware is actually how you disempower the story/evaluation and empower yourself instead. Feeling your feelings empowers you.

Now imagine you share this story with another. You walk over to your partner or friend and ask if they have a moment. You ask, "Is it a good time for me to share something that has come up for me?" Let them know you are vulnerable in sharing. If they say yes, then you may say something like, "Remember when you spoke to so-and-so, and you were both laughing really loud and enjoying each other very much? Well, I just wanted you to know I felt left out. I began to feel jealous and had thoughts of, what if that means I'm not special anymore?" The listener would add in either an appreciation for your honesty, or an inquiry into what you may need or how it could have looked different.

Right there in that moment, the story has begun to lose its grip on you! You have just switched from disconnecting from others to creating a more intimate connection by being transparent. Nowhere in this new conversation are you saying something is wrong. You aren't blaming anyone or even asking for anything to be different. You are simply being authentic and owning your story.

Through my years of learning, teaching and living in intentional communities, I have witnessed over and over again how transparency helped create deeper bonds and a very safe environment to feel all the emotions and feelings we experience.

Plus, it encourages and empowers healthier, more vibrant and juicier relationships with ourselves and others.

Being transparent means you reveal your inner self, your internal experiences. You share the feelings, which arise in the moment, about personal matters or conflicts with another person. You connect in transparency, rather than hide in your story playing out in your head. Yes, that means you share your vulnerabilities and fears, it means you share your desires and points of view. Remember you are learning to share just for the sake of sharing and practicing transparency, not with the intention of getting something. Your voice, words and feelings are energy. When you hold them back, or push them down and judge them that's where the trouble begins. It creates distress in our bodies, our relationships and our businesses. Being transparent means there is no more hiding. It is a chance to finally share all of who you really are with others. WOW! Isn't that exciting?

## The Bottomless Pit of Processing

Sometimes there are circumstances that trigger a trauma response. You may experience this as an endless cyclic conversation of revisiting a painful incident or conflict. The emotional story grows, and with it grows the need to express this emotional story, and every time it's retold, it is like rubbing salt in an open wound. Sometimes this can start as a simple conversation expressing one's feelings and can balloon into hours of processing why you or your partner feel a certain way. It can also look like a loop cycle where there is a habit of continually coming back to that same conversation without a means to an end. There is a lack of resolution and proactivity in moving forward. This is different than sharing transparently.

Most of us have experienced this. It is one of those perfectly human moments. And it's okay. However, I'm sure you're ready to find your way out of those endless cycles when they happen.

Such episodes confirm that there likely is a need that is going repeatedly unmet, and has been for a really long time. It might even be a need that has been going unmet since way before this relationship began. Remember, this happens in family dynamics, friendships and with colleagues.

Another possibility is that getting caught in the loop is an old pattern of creating a false sense of safety. When the mind gets absorbed in endlessly analyzing something, it blocks the ability to feel, and those uncomfortable feelings can be pushed down without you even realizing it.

Someone might get stuck in the same conversation again and again so they don't have to move forward. Not moving forward means they don't risk losing what they have, meanwhile keeping themselves attached to this story like an old worn out security blanket.

The idea that clinging to the present or denying our deepest feelings and needs can get us what we want is so far from the truth. If we step back as the observer and look at such an experience, we can see that it is suffocating the person who is stuck in the trauma response, keeping them frozen, and starving the relationship at hand.

What do you do when you or someone you relate with gets stuck in endless processing? Breaking a loop requires the one stuck in it to do a lot of self inquiry, get radically honest with themselves in regards to what they need in their environment to feel safe. Sometimes it is hard to see when you're so deep in the thick of the forest. Often it means reaching out to a professional at times to be a guide for you to remember your higher truth and transition the emotional memory.

If the people involved are skilled in communication and able to be present, they can begin to break the cycle simply by acknowledging that it is happening, and owning it. Awareness is always a first step.

Own it. Acknowledge what in the environment may be a triggering factor. What is not working for you? Continuously showing up late for a date, answering the phone when you are wanting to create more connection and presence, making executive decisions without including you are a few examples of behaviors that could be triggering. See if you can make a request that will eliminate the trigger for you. As well, unpack what beliefs are coming up based on the experience.

For example, if someone has a habit of showing up late you might request a phone call from them updating you on any changes instead of just showing up later than you expected. You may request that you and your colleagues have weekly check-in's, or that you increase the number of check-in's prior to making a big decision to make sure you are all on the same page.

What happens when your partner or people you are relating to are not willing or wanting or able to meet your request? This is the edgier part. It can be easy to get lost in the idea that they must meet your request, When that happens, your request becomes a demand, and all you actions begin to feel like a demand of sorts (remember that agreements can be cages). You start loosing ground, feeling panicked, scared, angry, and your fight or flight response throws you right back into the endless processing cycle.

In this case, you must change the relationship dynamic somehow. Get clear on what your bottom line is, what can stay the same and what will have to change. A bottom line may be "I will only listen to your feelings when they're communicated from a self-responsible place and for a maximum of 15 minutes, but I will not process those feelings with you." This shows that you are clear on what you need and want but are still open to the experience of the other person.

If you cannot sustain your bottom line, and professional help is not working or is out of reach, it may be best to cut the cord. Contrary to the popular belief that we need to take care of and fix the other person, compassionately cutting the cord is the biggest act of love you might be able to offer to the relationship and the people involved. If it is an intimate relationship let your beloved know how much you love them, and how much you believe they deserve to feel safe and to really get their requests and needs met. Know you are sharing this even though you may not be the one to meet those needs.

Remember that relationships change over time, and that we transition in and out of phases of a relationship all the time. Refusing to get stuck in an endless cycle of processing can serve as one of those transitions. We will more fully explore how to transition a relationship in an upcoming chapter.

## Asking For What You Want

How often have you really, really wanted something, but your old belief system told you that you did not deserve it? Or, afraid of what others may think, you held yourself back from asking for it? Maybe at some point you really wanted a meal made a certain way? You had a preference on a date yet settled without speaking your mind? How many times have you held yourself back from sharing a sexual desire or fantasy?

I was sitting outside of the market with a friend laughing and talking as we prepared to share an intentional day out in the forest. All of a sudden, a man who was giving away the most scrumptious looking chocolate cake approached us. With a smile on his face it was obvious it was his joy to share. As he approached with two pieces of cake asking us if we would like a piece. I declined, but my friend's eyes widened as she said "hmmmm" with a bit of hesitation. Then she asked softly if she could please have a smaller piece of what was on the plate. Due to her low tone and hesitant voice, the man didn't hear her. When he asked her to repeat herself, she casually said "never mind." She really wanted the scrumptious cake, yet felt like a hassle in her request.

Personally, I love championing for what people desire especially when they hold back from asking for what they want. I quickly spoke up. "Sir, my friend here would love a bit of the big piece. Would it be okay if she just took that little corner that is on the plate?" He said "of course," as she reached out with joy to receive the sweet, sensual bit of chocolate deliciousness.

I believe that if you want something you should ask for it because you deserve it. You might get a no or yes, but you will never know unless you express exactly what you want. My friend did not want the full piece of cake but she did want a small bite. This example was a painfully common illustration of where so many people are in life and relationships. How many times have you really wanted something, and found yourself holding back thinking that you don't deserve it or it's not that important or that people will think you are crazy or selfish?

We know life would not have ended if she did not get that piece of cake. Yet she desired to have it! How empowering it is to use your voice, and fully receive in life and love, even love for cake. When we settle and don't ask for what we want in the form of clear, honest communication we begin to feel resentment. We get frustrated and experience a lack of confidence and creative expression.

Asking for what you want can have a lot of confusing attributes. When do I ask, is the other person available to listen, will I be rejected, made fun of, will I get yelled at or worse if I say the wrong thing? Sometimes the moment leading up to asking can feel like the scariest, most nerve wrecking experience. When you ask for something you desire, there will be a degree of vulnerability to it.

A key to easing your anxiety around asking is to re-frame the way you experience being vulnerable. Examine any nervousness and re-frame it as enthusiasm or excitement at the prospect of getting what you want, it loosens that knot of fears into fluttering butterflies. The vulnerability in itself can be seen as a win because you are choosing to be fully expressed, fully authentic no matter what. Another great re-frame!

### *How to Ask*

Your ask stands a much better chance of landing well if you prepare yourself by remembering these ideas.

**Breathe** — Prepare yourself by taking a few deep diaphragmatic breaths, make sure you have the appropriate time to express your ask and remind yourself just to be you.

**Be transparent** — I love being real honest before I ask. If I am nervous, I will begin the conversation by acknowledging this and telling the person or people I am asking that I am nervous. "I have had something on my mind and have been holding it back because I feel so nervous to ask, I am concerned about what you would think or how it would come across." When you own what you are feeling rather than pretending it will relax the nervous system, you will feel calmer and the other person or people will also feel more relaxed and safe with you. Transparency creates connection.

**Make a request not a demand** — You want the ask to be inviting, welcoming. You are seeking to be heard and to create a win/win experience. Demands will only put up walls of defense that keep the receiver from hearing what you are asking for.

**Leave expectations and the need to convince someone else outside of the room** — Just be yourself and share from the heart. This is crucial because not everyone will be available to agree with your ask or show up the way you expect and want them too.

Choosing the Best Time to Ask:

1. Have a good night sleep and feel rested.
2. Make sure your blood sugar is level and you have been nourished. Don't have the conversation after a busy work day while driving home in rush hour. That would be an example of when not to ask.
3. Be grounded. Make sure you are not scattered in a million directions.
4. Make sure you have adequate time to ask and space to have a conversation. Depending on the topic of your ask, you will need to be the judge of how much time is needed.
5. Be aware of the state of the person or people you are asking. If you see they are exhausted, haven't eaten all day or are in a rush, it's your responsibility to make an empowered decision to reschedule the conversation for a time when everyone can be fully present.

I remember years ago a Kabbalistic teacher I was studying with gave an example of how asking is actually sharing and in some ways showing love and kindness to others. That really resonated when I unpacked the topic to see how it became an act of kindness.

When you ask, you are inviting in a certain sense of intimacy and trust. When you ask, you are offering an opportunity for another person to be of service and share more of themselves. When you ask for something such as to spend time with someone, have a work date, or to be touched in a certain way, or to share a sexual fantasy, you are sharing with the other how attracted you are to them and that you would like more of them.

Asking is a gift because it opens the door to knowing yourself, and another more. It empowers and inspires new conversations.

## Communication Reminder

In a busy world, it might seem easy to let the quality of your communication take the sidelines. But that's not a winning strategy. If you are less than satisfied with the quality of your relationship, if you notice that you have a tendency to become more anxious in certain conversations and then explode on the other person or implode on yourself, then it's time to put communication back in the spotlight. Remember to be patient with yourself and others, and to practice as often as you are able. Intentional dialog is a skill that requires greater presence, mindfulness, curiosity, and compassion. We all have the need to be loved and understood; good communication is essential.

# Meeting the Needs of All in the Relationship

Living in these human bodies offers universal human needs and feelings. Denying this basic fundamental truth can wreak emotional havoc and create separation in our relationships. Human needs need to be met in some fashion.

I have had a number of clients, many of them men, come to me because they are feeling trapped, uncomfortable in their bodies, like a bird in a cage, or a dog with a muzzle. They feel like their solar plexus is in a noose, their chests are tight, shoulders to their ears.

For these men, work, activities and sex have become mechanical—a way to run farther away from their own selves. Sex has become all about getting off, and lacks intimate bonding. And upon that soulless ejaculation, they feel a yearning for something more.

What swells up in these men are feelings of confusion, confusion about their role as a man. They feel lost in a world where sex is a mere soulless act of raw physical penetration. And they are walking around guarded, asking "how do I get back to the place where my spirit and sex are one, where I feel safe to be held and caressed? How do I open my heart, open myself to being touched, to crying, to being radically who I am, with grace, with presence and with ease? How do I get to that place where I feel safe with the raw passion of my wild sexuality, where I am welcomed and met equally by my partner?"

These empty voids are often left vacant to be filled with an addiction whether it be addiction to over-working, eating, shopping, self loathing, pornography or drugs. Often, these men end up in a long series of unhealthy relationships, waiting for their partner to fulfill them. This feeling does not only pertain to men, as many women have similar journeys to reconnect with the power of their sacred fire.

This way of living and relating feels like a painful dependence on the people around you. This level of codependency often weighs on the relationships, suffocating the people within them. How often does your confidence and self-expression depend on receiving someone else's approval? How often, as an adult, have you been confused by your own emotional needs?

Relational dysfunction grows out of a garden that has not received adequate nutrients: a baby not getting enough touch and attention; a child being told over and over again to be quiet. In order to make that garden grow and thrive, its needs have to be met. That raises the question, in a relationship, who is responsible for meeting my needs?

This answer may seem complicated especially when in a coupled relationship, however the truth of the matter is you are ultimately responsible for meeting your own needs. This means that no matter what your partner chooses that you are responsible for your happiness, joy, peace and creating environments that fuel you.

Now with that being said, if two or more people enter into a relationship, each party is, to a certain degree, agreeing to be present to the needs of the relationship. They choose to plant a garden together and they know that for the garden to grow and thrive they must both contribute to watering it.

The complication begins to happen when there is an emotional enmeshment and you or your partner (or friend or colleague) begin to threaten the relationship or the people in it because they are not fulfilling your needs. That threat takes the form of blaming, pointing the finger and adopting the idea that, by signing up for this beautiful field of shared relating, you are responsible for the other, like parents are to their young.

When did the idea come into play that a relationship is about the other person meeting our needs or us meeting their needs 100%? Did the relationship paradigm revert us back to children and looking at our partners or even our friends as if they were our parents?

Have you caught yourself thinking or saying "you don't make me feel sexy anymore, you make me feel unhappy and frustrated"? Have you been angry because the sex has stopped, the soft intimate touch has lessened and you find yourself blaming your partner because they aren't doing something you want?

What you are feeling may be true, such as feeling unhappy, frustrated and angry. However when the blame game starts it turns into a game of manipulation, working to convincing your partner or friends to give you what you want even if your partner does not want to. I have been there, in the moments of feeling uncentered, drained and grasping for that which is closest to me. I get it. And you can imagine how awful this feels for you and your partner or friend. Do you feel this would make you any more attractive, or open their hearts more to fulfill your need? When you manipulate another into meeting your needs, the outcome is more disconnect. And if your partner does act to fulfill your needs, and is feeling resistance, the actions they take are often mechanical.

What's more, making someone else responsible for your needs will leave you tired out, which will lead to a lack of intimacy, lack of attraction, lack of feeling attractive, and can sometimes even go as far as someone feeling turned off by the other person and craving their own space.

When you feel full, the relationship automatically feels full and that attracts. If you, your partner and your friends focused on meeting all of your own needs to feel at peace, secure, attractive and sexy, it creates more space and vitality to share more emotional intimacy. If it is a sexual relationship and both are in full agreement often the affection and sex you desired will happen organically because you both feel fueled by your own life choices.

For a moment let go of the idea that you are someone else's responsibility and put yourself in their shoes. Would it feel draining if someone was forcing you to feel a certain way? Would it make you want to stay in that situation or leave?

To often people jump from relationship to relationship to get their needs met, to get that void filled. But they fall into the same trap every time by making the other the source of their happiness. Eventually the same thing happens, the manipulation starts, the fatigue and resentment set in and viola, off to the next one.

Throughout the book you have been offered ideas and practices on how to take radical self responsibility for your own feelings and needs, to fuel your own worth and to embrace your invaluable self. Stop resisting and start embracing what fuels you outside of the other person. When you step back into your personal power, there will be more to share with others!

When it comes to meeting your needs that can only be fulfilled by sharing with another, take a lesson from business. At the start of a big project, there is always communication around obligations. It usually looks like a contract, but can also be lists of to-do's and deliverables. There is a clear communication of who is doing what and the people involved agree upon it. If they can't come to an agreement that mutually satisfies all the needs, then they do not go forward with a project that won't bear fruit. Use your communication skills in your relationships to let others know what your needs are. If you cannot come to an agreeable way to meet each other's needs, it may be time to reflect, take solo time and revisit if this is the right relationship.

## *Imbalanced Giving*

Maybe you were raised to be a giver. You have a tendency to give and give and give. There is nothing wrong with giving; you may experience absolute joy from giving. You may feel so fueled when you experience someone else being nourished and happy. Giving and sharing is a powerful important exchange of energy when the giver's cup is full.

The more we receive the more we have to actually give. Think of it like pouring into a cup until it is overflowing into another cup beneath, which then overflows into another and another.

When it happens like this, even receiving becomes giving. Imagine you had someone who continually brought you gifts and you continued to refuse them. By receive you are gifting another person the joy and benefits of giving as well.

For some, though, giving is a running away response. This would be true if it is difficult for you to receive because the attention makes you uncomfortable, or you believe that you are unworthy. Over time this would lead to imbalance and functioning in a way that hid parts of your beautiful self.

I want to red-flag some of the things that pop up when you are giving more than you have capacity for. The degree varies from person to person, and it can shift depending on your emotional, physical, psychological, and energetic state. If you are giving beyond our capacity, you might experience any of these things:

- Feeling anxious or agitated.
- Getting caught up in emotional stories when you give.
- A rising level of expectations and frustration replacing the joy you once had at giving.

- Wanting to spend time alone and then feeling lonely when you are on your own.

I want to address those of you who feel pleasure from giving. Know this is something different than over-giving. I love the wheel analogy as it is one of my favorites because it is so clear. If part of the wheel was you actively giving, you felt alive when you gave and witnessed another's pleasure and it may mean you are one of those people who needs less self care. We are all so very different in our capacity levels. The other half of the wheel was you simply surrendering, going into a tune-up, recharging your battery. You wouldn't constantly drive your Mazaratti or Tesla endlessly without sending it into the car spa, right?! If only half of that wheel gets attention eventually the wheel gets out of balance, which makes for a less-than-quality ride.

Even if you need less time to recharge, being in the receiving mode simply to receive without giving is invaluable for a few reasons. It means sharing a new level of vulnerability which only happens in complete surrender. It is the moment you let go of control. Sometimes being the giver all the time is a programed state (not bad, just programed). It is what you grew up seeing and doing so it feels really good. We want to develop the soft vulnerable side of surrendering in addition to your capacity to give. You do this in receiving.

Surrendering to receive not only gives you more capacity to give again but you are ultimately giving to your partner by being in the receiving role. Remember how good it felt to give? It is such a gift to allow our loved ones, friends, colleagues and partners to explore their own giving wheel. By receiving, you allow someone to know another part of you, a vulnerable part.

I remember being in Mexico for my 44th birthday. We gathered a few close friends to share in ceremony for a few days. I placed myself in a birthing process through meditation, connecting to the sea as if it were the womb and entering into a Temazcal Mayan sweat lodge on the pacific ocean. We shared wisdom together, and at sunset, we came out of the womb space acknowledging it as a form of re-birth, and rested on the beach watching the whales migrating with their young. This year was ever more special as I would be sharing it with my beloved who flew in from California to spend four days with me.

This year the intention was to follow tradition by entering into another ceremony. Unfortunately I became violently sick the day before the ceremony. Life had something completely different in store. The vulnerability in sharing space when I'm extremely sick is an edge for me. I was vomiting non-stop for nearly 24 hours and my beloved made it clear he came there to be with me and felt taking care of me was such a gift because as it stood, I was unable to do anything for myself. Now I see myself as great at receiving but this was edgy for me. I recall feeling guilty every time I needed something. I needed help walking from the couch to the bed, and to the bathroom because I was so weak. Somehow, wrapped inside the unpleasantness of being sick was a beautiful gift: a new powerful bond between us. I was dropped completely into that vulnerable surrender.

I want you to take some time in your daily practice to reflect on your pattern of giving and receiving with others. Reflect on these questions:

- Is it easier for you to give than to receive?
- Do you like to be in control, to take the lead? And it is more challenging for you otherwise? This may show up as talking very quickly, holding body tension, breathing stuck in the chest and tension in the solar plexus.
- What ways do you enjoy receiving? Do you receive more than you give?

# Sharing Your Sex

I am writing this chapter while on a week long solo retreat. I have just completed a one hour Vipassana meditation, and as I sit here and write I feel my body so open, so available to life. As my eyes close I feel the pumping of my blood through my veins, the temperature changes within my body, the softness and tensions of various parts of my musculature. It feels as if life is entering my heart and caressing my sex. I am in tune with the subtle movements of the trees, the soft caress of the wind. My ears are so sensitive to the sweet sounds of the song birds, the buzzing of the bees, and the crows in the distance. Vitality, connection, information and wisdom. I am in my eyes, being penetrated by nature. I have said yes to joining in divine partnership with what life offers. And although I am physically alone and in complete stillness, I feel very sexually alive.

*Soulful Sex*

To be sexually liberated we must approach sex from a holistic viewpoint. It is not a mere physical act where our genitals are touched to the point of orgasm. In a soulful sex experience, where the orgasm becomes less of the focus of the pure ravishment, it transmutes into higher states and potential experiences. I believe having a one-pointed goal has become a distraction from cultivating a rich, deep relationship with sexuality and the penetrative reality of nature and life. What would be possible if you were to stop seeking the quick pleasure and bliss, the getting drunk and distracted on the surface of pleasure, and dive to the depths?

Yes, orgasm is a part of our sexual experience and has many health benefits, but let it not be your agenda. What if you could feel that orgasmic energy, those sensations that build up to orgasm, all the way through a sexual encounter without depending on having an orgasm or outward response? I am not suggesting you stop orgasming as it is part of our nature and wellbeing. I am, however, inviting you to uncover more and broaden your perspective.

Throughout this book you have explored ways to do just this, to get more in your body, to peel away the emotional burdens of the past, to start to find greater stillness, to start to communicate more with your body, your heart, your energy, your sex. You have richer skills to also share this new found presence, awareness, and communication with others. Now you have the opportunity to apply it to your sex.

This is truly unleashing spirit in your sex life. This is where you are bringing your potent, rooted turn-on to share with another who matches you in that rooted, emotionally clear turn-on without depending on physical penetration. It is a shamanic journey in itself where you actually gain more by your willingness to lose everything.

When you show up in such reverence and devotion to yourself, your sex is a part of that self, it mirrors how you show up in relation to others. You naturally begin to feel and see life differently. From this place of allowing life to make love to you in every moment, you move with a sense of grace, connection, presence, compassion and even a fierce vulnerability. There is power in this. Yet a power that lives in your center that is not one of forcing or manipulating but one of understanding.

Sex has just shifted from hard, physical forceful penetration to ravishment, to whole bodied, spiritual penetration that touches your soul. A sexual union where even the slightest of touches puts you into greater connection with your higher self. Thought gives way to presence. You and your partner dance as if you are one. With each breath you feel life pouring more life into you. You feel liberated and safe within your own inner security where you may give voice to all your desires and fantasies. However, you never lose yourself for an instant. You find yourself the more you allow yourself to disappear into a formlessness that is only possible when you unleash spirit in your sex life.

### Cultural Conditioning Around Sex

For most of us, unleashing your spirit in your sex life is easier said than done. We have been dragged along by cultural conditioning in regards to what relationships and sex should look like.

You likely weren't given a course of in-depth sexuality education which included the topics of consent, how to navigate desire, conscious touch, and how to use your sexual parts so you experience the most pleasure. You likely weren't raised to learn to relate to your own body and another person's body beyond reproductive biology. Am I getting warm? Well guess what, you are not alone. Most of the world has lived in this same paradigm.

This paradigm isn't working for us. As Christopher Ryan notes in his book, Sex At Dawn, we have a "sweet tooth for sex," but we have not successfully integrated that desire for sex into our culture in a healthy way.

*Yes, something is seriously wrong. The American Medical Association reports that some 42 percent of American women suffer from sexual dysfunction, while Viagra breaks sales records year after year. Worldwide, pornography is reported to rake in anywhere from fifty-seven to a hundred-billion-dollars annually. In the United States, it generates more revenue than CBS, NBC, and ABC combined, and more than all professional football, baseball, and basketball franchises. According to U.S. News and World Report, "Americans spend more money at strip clubs than at Broadway, off-Broadway, regional and nonprofit theaters, the opera, the ballet and jazz and classical music performances—combined.*[5]

Sex education in the west has for decades focused on fear based education. We are told sex is scary because it leads to disease and unwanted pregnancy. We are taught how to avoid sex instead of how to navigate your sexuality in an empowered way. Sex is actually a pleasurable experience, but you would never know it from the way we teach it. It is an experience which has the potential to last for hours (A 2005 study found that sex lasts just 5.4 minutes on average[6]). Were you aware of that? Yes your desire, your pleasure and the expression of it are fucking beautiful!

Our cultural treatment of sex has lead not just to a lack of fulfillment with one's self but also to disconnection in relationships, and to burdening people with shame and guilt. A relationship with sexual dysfunction and misuse of sexual power feels like prison a sentence.

Living in such disconnection with our bodies and their abilities leaves many yearning for a connection that they just don't know how to create. This has lead to so much confusion because nothing was shared with you about the depths of your body or the options you have to make that connection happen.

---

[5]Christopher Ryan, Sex at Dawn [Harper, 2010, USA]
[6]Waldinger MD, Quinn P, Dilleen M, Mundayat R, Schweitzer DH, Boolell M, "A Multinational Population Survey of Intravaginal Ejaculation Latency Time," The Journal of Sexual Medicine, Vol. 2, Issue 4 (2005): 492–97. https://www.ncbi.nlm.nih.gov/pubmed/16422843

Exploring kink, recreational sex for pleasure, gender identity, and sexual orientation are natural parts of the human experience.

Why is the world so focused on the so called dangers of sex, forgetting the pleasure? With such a skewed focus, the world, your world, may have felt sexually dysfunctional at times.

There is a middle point in sexuality. Society has a tendency to fall into one of the extremes, either trying to completely suppress our enjoyment of sex, or allowing it to be the source of violence. But there is a pleasure zone of liberated sexuality. The expression of our sexuality includes love and pleasure. It means we communicate how we want our lovers to touch us. It includes consideration for how we live in relation to all beings and how to inter-relate, feel intimacy and express desires.

In order to dive into the infinite ocean of your sexuality and share the mystery in such an open way with another you must be willing to get vulnerable. For men, or those who walk in a more masculine essence, it requires letting go of the feelings of inadequacy and removing the idea that you are the feminine's savior. When you move beyond such an idea the Manic Mind lets go and you gain the ability to be more present. This also brings more freedom to the dance between lovers.

Be receptive to your partner while they are accessing their own pleasure and even possibly inviting you to touch them or penetrate them or kiss them in a different way than what you have been doing. Can you surrender to the moment knowing that anything could happen? You can only access this depth when you are willing to let go of it all.

For women, or those who consider themselves to be of a feminine gender, or the feminine part of you, diving into this infinite ocean requires you to fully love yourself. Do you know what it means and feels like to make love to yourself? Are you willing to pleasure yourself and feel your confidence in your sensual body? When those of us in our feminine gender role feel this embodied confidence it is from here that we will fully open up and blossom into our pleasure to be shared with another.

For everyone, it means shedding our cultural condition around sexuality and intimacy. Let your inner sacred fire light the way.

## My Journey Through Cultural Conditioning

Finding those first steps is not easy, even if you let your sacred fire show you the path. There were a lot of twists and turns on my own journey before I was able to really listen to what my body was telling me.

I loved embracing my sexual beingness, riding that dangerous edge with my sexual energy and exploring the vast world of pleasure through my teens. Even with the joy of curiosity I had for my turn-on, I chose to wait to have sexual intercourse until I had my first "real" boyfriend at age 18. By real I mean we had a serious relationship and called each other boyfriend and girlfriend.

Even though I was quite aware of my sexuality at a much younger age, I did not share the fullness of my virginity until I was 18 for no other reason than I always felt that when someone was going to penetrate me in such a way and enter my body that there needed to be a certain amount of presence and care.

Now my boyfriend at the time and I had a great relationship, and it was clear to us both that I thoroughly enjoyed sex much more than he did at the time. We would joke that at 20 years old, it was like he was 60. He understood this and we laughed about it. After 3 years something began to blossom in me. Something new which I had not felt during our relationship. I started becoming curious to other men.

My sexual life force and connection pulsed through me and I yearned to be met in this way. I yearned to have a partner to share this wordless communication with. We loved each other and we had different needs at the time. In my twenties I did not have the communication tools that I do now. And they may not have helped as much as we needed because I had not yet developed the skill to understand all the parts of my emotional body.

I remember one night being at a party with all my friends, and there was this one guy there... The excitement felt electric to me, the euphoric chemicals that flood the brain with new attraction were lighting me up, and next thing I knew we were making out. When that magic moment ended I was instantly overcome with an immense amount of guilt and shame. The instant arrival of weighty guilt mixing with all that oxytocin—the love drug—made for an awfully confusing mix of feelings.

Without the skills to talk about it, and so much shame and guilt, I couldn't escape the feeling that I did not deserve a relationship and that I needed to be punished. I went home, and the next day ended the relationship with my boyfriend even though it's not what he wanted. For the next three years sex became a power tool for me. It was a way of punishment. I used sex in dishonoring my body and spirit, gradually forgetting about myself, what I enjoyed and the vibrancy of who I was at my core. I wanted to push my feelings down to suffocate the guilt, to hopefully, no longer experience it. All the sensitivity I had for life began to slip away. Sex became empty, I allowed the men I was with to do anything they wanted to me. I allowed my voice to be muffled. The years started to numb me out until finally there was no other choice but to stop. Sex slowed down, yet this was around the same period of my life when I was pushing myself beyond my limits in my drive as a bodybuilder. I have no doubt that adding sexual self-punishment to my overtaxed exercise regimen contributed to my collapse. It felt like my life was over, but it was the start to actually living!

I allowed this experience to be my teacher. I went through nearly seven years of celibacy cultivating a new relationship with my body, mind and spirit. I knew it was time and that I was the only one who had the power within to change my life and my relationship with my body and sex.

I want you to know that you don't have to wait until something so big knocks you on the head or drops you to your knees. I don't believe you have to wait, which is why you are here reading this book. My story unfolded as it did all because I was ridden with intense emotional shame and guilt. I did not fully understand that being attracted to other people is a natural human response, and that if I had had the voice to communicate, it would have allowed the soulful sex to expand in my life.

## Sex as a Vehicle of Communication

As with so many things in relationships, communication is the key to deepening our sexual connection. Communication goes far beyond the common use of words which we use in social conversations or at a dinner party.

We are communicating in every moment through the way our body moves, the tempo of our own breath, through our sighs and gentle moans. even physiological changes, like when our body temperature changes or perspiration happens, are a form of communication.

In that light, you can think of sex itself as a form of

communication. The body has a unique language, and the heightened states which are reached through sexual arousal open the doors to such a non-verbal language, which I believe is an important part of our nature, one which deserves attention and understanding.

Of course, there is an importance for clear verbal communication of your desires, boundaries, fantasies, etc. But there is also a place for this non-verbal platform of sex-as-a-language to be explored. When one of these forms of communication (explicit verbal and implicit physical) is disregarded or not understood as an important component of intimacy, the magic of soulful sex is lost.

I spoke earlier in the book about how meditation is a powerful tool to access greater states of sensitivity and arousal at a very deep level. This is where sexual arousal, or turn-on as I like to call it, moves beyond the physical act of penetrative sex and expands into a full body turn-on which you can switch on at anytime. This means living in a heightened state of awareness, feeling more connected to what your body and spirit needs and having a healthy vital glow to you which enriches everything you experience.

You may have experienced moments where your form of communication shifted from verbal to non-verbal, to body-speak. You may have had a moment or two where your mind has disappeared and your body felt electrified on high sensory awareness.

It is in such a moment of shared heightened sexual activation that we go deeper into the sensation, and there is more to explore. When the two sharing in such a field have developed such awareness it is a learning exploration, of not just our own desires and feelings but also of how deeper parts of our being respond to various motions, energies, words, and touch. It can seem like a whole universe is opening up within us.

## Your Sacred Fire

In part one, The Relationship With One's Self, we talked about ways to get your sexual energy flowing by deepening the relationship you have with your own sexuality. We used meditation, self pleasuring, conscious touch and other forms of exploration and self-inquiry to really juice up that sacred fire. Remember, that energy belongs to you, it comes from you. And you have the opportunity to let it shine when you bring it into a sexual relationship with someone else.

I find that when one's energy is open and flowing efficiently, that they are also feeling their own arousal state. We talked about this in the section on Mindfulness and Self Pleasure. I described that arousal state as subtle, gentle flowing energy currents running through the body, making you aware of your sexual root, softening your heart and opening your mind.

When two energies come together which are grounded, centered and emotionally clear, even without physical penetration, they mingle in such a way as to heighten their sexual energy, to merge energies, to make love.

Watch the life all around you—a hummingbird receiving nectar from a flower, bees pollinating, the way we laugh during a playful conversation—sexual energy is there, and it extends far beyond merely engaging in sexual intercourse.

Within this new way of relating, commitment is always present. The healthy commitment to show up, and to empower healthy relating rather than disempowering and supporting fear. It means bringing that energy with you and opening up to share it with another. Sexuality, sexual energy and your turn-on is yours, your gift to share and be in right relationship with when you feel called. It is from this overflow of sexual energy that we empower our relationships, we bring them to fullness, rather than needing to get filled up by them.

## *Owning Your Sexual Independence*

Bringing your sexual energy into a relationship goes hand-in-hand with taking ownership for your own pleasure, and of your sexual independence. As strange as it might seem, really owning these things will bring new heights to the sexual connection you create with another.

Have you ever gone into a relationship or on a date with a huge agenda or expectation that the person you were going on a date with was going to get you off, do it just right and get you so turned on? Or maybe your experience was the other way around: you went in with such high expectations that it was your job to please them, bring them to climax or get them to ejaculate, that you were so much in your head, so occupied with that idea that your body certainly did not feel the fullness of pleasure it could have?

I had a client, Cathy, who had a lifetime of challenges in orgasm. As I began to mentor her, she shared with me stories about being not-so-present in her body, that during sex the lower belly and vagina area often felt contracted and tense. When Cathy went on dates she had a strong expectation that she needed to please her partner and needed to do so by orgasming. That kind of thinking only added to the stress and the disconnection Cathy felt inside. You can imagine how this became like a domino effect on the entire pleasure experience.

This particular case was all about feeling safe to slow down, to feel again, to feel safe in her body. It also meant returning to her power and having the ability to say yes only to what felt right for her body and to say no when it did not. Cathy's journey was about feeling again, using her voice, and feeling safe to do so.

You can see how having an expectation around sex limited her ability to dive deeply into it and enjoy it. Giving up the expectation that she had to orgasm for their partner and adopting the idea that they could have an orgasm for their own pleasure, and could direct their lover in helping them achieve it deepened the experience for both of them.

When caught up in a relationship or a sexual exploration with another it can be easy to sometimes forget your own sexual truths, all that awareness your accessed through exploring your sovereign sexual self. Your sexual partner may want sex when you don't, they may want touch in ways you might not prefer, they may also check-out and get caught up in their sexual agenda. It is important to remember your are invaluable and your unique sexual expression is worthy in every way. Rather than relinquishing your sexual self, your preferences, share them, talk about them. Use those communication skills, ideally before you're tearing your clothes off in the bedroom, as once penetrative sex has started it becomes much more of a sensitive subject. This does not mean that you don't share and use your voice in the bed, but make time for longer conversations to happen before the sex happens.

I'll give you an example of how owning your pleasure and using your communication skills can really up your connection. In the midst of sexual passion, the masculine role, or man gets lost in the constant hard thrusting. He will think you are also enjoying this unless you share differently. If it doesn't feel good, or if it hurts, stop! Rather than abruptly saying that it hurts or stop that and do this, why not say gently "I'd love to explore playing with different rhythms of penetrations. I would love to feel your cock slowly enter me fully and maybe just see what it feels like to play with only the tip of the penis penetrating." You are turning your desires into an invitation. Share what feels really good about it, what not so good and develop a game of getting to know each other's sexual self rather than settling and checking into unconscious sex which leads to frustration, disconnection and harm in the long run.

Owning your pleasure is a two way street. In the first part of this book we worked on the ever important relationship with the self. Every component within this book, all your wonderful journeys and exercises you are exploring are ways to cultivate more awareness, sensitivity and pleasure in your body and peace in your mind. This is the case when you are exploring your sexuality on your own, and it is also the case when you are sharing your sexual energy with another.

Remember to put your compassionate communication skills to work here. You and your lover are really just desiring to love each other and enjoy each other, however, it is perfectly human to have differences, likes and dislikes. This is why it is important to own not just your desires in sex, but you need to own your independence too.

This is a big one, especially within a relationship structure. Often such an idea may be easier to grasp when you are single or not in a pair bonded relationship sharing your life with someone extensively. You can see that if you are casually dating or have lovers that come in and out, your sexual independence makes sense. Right? You hopefully are getting to know what you like and dislike, what turns you on, what turns you off, and what your sexual boundaries are. You also choose to engage sexually with others who are sexually similar.

If you are in a long term relationship where you have been

evolving and growing together, the initial sexual chemistry and similarities that were there upon the first kiss might be shifting after ten years or more. Shifting does not mean something bad, remember. But because you are different today your sexual preferences may be different too. You may enjoy sex now at mid-day instead of having an all-nighter. You may have noticed a decrease in sex drive after having children, or getting signed on for an epic job promotion.

I remember a period in a relationship where I started feeling my partner and I enter into the "mature love" phase. This happens after the new relationship energy (NRE) fades. NRE is the chemical high of first meeting. Mature love for me took on more of a rich meditative quality. There was so much tenderness, finishing each other's sentences, sharing intimate closeness. Our lovemaking became multidimensional though our all-nighters became less frequent.

Owning our sexual independence comes through sexual liberation. What would you do if you were in a long, loving relationship, you and your partner adored each other and have a couple of beautiful children, but it became clear that at this point in your life that your sexual needs and desires were completely different from one another? This is quite common which is why we see so much nonconsensual action in the world of relating and a lot of shame and disconnection building upon it.

I want to invite in sexual independence through sexual liberation. I remember Doug, a past client who shared with me that he and his partner had a conversation about their sexual needs and desires. She had many physiological changes since bearing children and he was a very fiery sexual person. They sat and declared their love for each other, and how much the relationship was a priority, so much that she owned her sexual independence and invited him to do the same. She said "If you feel you need more sexual expression I am a yes to you going and having these needs met elsewhere."

You may already feel the judgments arising as you're reading this. I want to acknowledge those judgments as this choice may not match your needs or style of relating. However, I want you to notice that those judgments often come from a place of conditioned beliefs and inner fear of your own. Be present with them and I invite you to keep reading with an open mind.

Being sexually liberated does not imply one is promiscuous or feels the need or desire to have sexual intercourse with a lot of people or all of the time. It is truly feeling at home, comfortable in the safest, coziest of relationships with one's owns sexuality. It means really owning one's desires, fantasies, fetishes and sexual uniqueness. It means expressing that sexual uniqueness openly without being overshadowed and holding back out of shame and embarrassment.

Sexual liberation is essential in a world where we are bred to wear masks of perfection, where sex is shamed and only meant for the bedroom, locked behind closed doors. I am hear to shout out that I prefer having sex everywhere but the bedroom! This adds an element of excitement and wild and unpredictability that is such a turn-on for many.

If we stay in the cages society has built for us rather than entering into this loving embrace and acknowledgment of our sexual liberation, everything in our world is affected. From the way we engage in business deals, to the way others feel around us, to the way we communicate, touch, relate and create.

*Ways Sex Can Be Damaging*

Sex is far bigger than I feel many realize. We aren't taught as children about the potential and bigness of our sexuality and life force. We have been exploring how to realize the best in all that potential power and how to overcome the emotional chaos it stirs up because of our cultural impact. When you're in a relationship and feeling alone, empty or angry, these feelings are often taken out on your partner. When that pours over into unhealthy control and manipulation in the bedroom, the bigness and power of our sexuality means the harm can permeate many levels.

I was having a conversation tonight with Alex, a young CEO who lived life at a very fast speed. He had a brilliant mind and had become very successful in his world. He thrived having such a fast paced mind, and loved mental stimulation. However, living in such a way, Alex barely had time to breathe. He lacked experiencing his fullest most liberated form of sex or the intimacy he knew was possible.

Alex was caught up in a persona that had it all together: clean cut, intelligent and successful in the business world. However, underneath he had wild desires, sexual fantasies and had a sexual curiosity which he was scared to express, with thoughts of being judged or his loved ones running in the other direction.

With a lifelong habit of living on the edge, which also meant a lot of pent up stress, Alex saw sex as a fun experience for stress relief. It became his band-aid. Just like going out with the guys to have a few drinks after work or hitting up the gym, even though these provide various levels of stress relief, they were keeping Alex at the superficial level hiding from deeper, sustainable shifts in his life.

In society sex has become a superficial escape, with many using it as a band-aid to cover over loneliness and pain, scared to be with the depth of who they are. While others us it as a medication that gives them a quick release of the stress they have created in an overstimulated life. Both are a means to numb and create radical separation at the core of who we are.

Suppressing one's desires creates a lack of understanding of one's self. Over time, bottling this up creates extreme levels of stress on the body and a world of declining health, covered in shame, waiting to erupt in sexual harm.

I say it is time to stop! Time to do things differently. Time for each human being to pause and say "Enough is enough!"

I too have used sex as a means to feel special and wanted, as well as a means for self-punishment. I understand how easy it can be to self-medicate through sexual pleasures and pains. It can seem all too easy to fill those emotional voids through sex.

After Alex decided to take on the tantric influenced practices, become more present with himself, access more stillness in the act of sex, he went on to share with me "I felt a little like I do during the peak of 'water fasts' ... euphoric in a way. Things smell better, sounds are more beautiful, and everything looks 'nicer.'"

There are many ways that touch can become harmful. The most obvious are sexual violence, rape and abuse. But sex can be damaging in much less noticeable ways, the harm can creep in from a place where there was none, or it can build up so slowly over the years that it goes undetected until it erupts in emotional catastrophe. I want to red-flag some of the harmful behaviors that often go unnoticed and unacknowledged.

- Having sex out of obligation.
- Doing a sexual act to please another when you don't want to or don't like the act.
- Having a pleasure agenda—a preformed idea about how someone else must feel pleasure with us, or the kinds of pleasure we want them to feel.

- Making someone else responsible for getting you off.
- Holding back expressing your sexual desires and fantasies to your partner out of fear or not wanting to know your partner's desires and fantasies.
- Cheating. Nonconsensual emotional and physical affairs.
- Not talking about STI's or safer sex out of embarrassment.
- Using sex as a means for stress release.

Ahimsa in sanskrit means non-harm. Non-harm to all beings including oneself. Self harm can take a lot of forms. It could be negative self talk or agreeing to do things you don't want to. Recall from my own story that for three years I used sex as a way to punish myself, and no good ever came from that punishment.

These harmful situations affect everyone involved negatively. Coercing or forcing someone else into a sexual act, or to fuel your desires or fantasies is skewed with unhealthy emotional toxins.

It is possible to experience what I would call an abusive relationship with your own sex. I would defined this by extreme lack of awareness, using sex to emotionally punish yourself or another, or engaging sexually when one is filled with rage, anger and discord which leads to manipulation or energetic disturbance.

If you notice these behaviors or patterns in your sex life, then it's time to get back to the basics. Go back to your self practice—the first stage in skill building—and get clear on your own desires, feelings and boundaries. Create a sacred space and explore what feelings you have around this issue, and what your needs are.

Then bring that back to your partner with engaging,

empowering heart-centered communication. Find a safe way to express what your feelings and needs are. Invite your partner in when you do it. Discuss what you can do together to make sex a more compassionate, passion filled, conscious playground and get the fun you truly desire.

### Pleasure Agenda

I want to single out and expand on one idea in the list of less obvious ways sex can be harmful. Have you ever been on a date, with a friend, lover or partner and felt the need for them to feel your pleasure, or for them to feel pleasure, or for you to make them feel pleasure? That is a pleasure agenda.

A pleasure agenda happens when you enter into a field with another person and place your agenda to feel pleasure on them, make yourself responsible for them feeling pleasure, or make them responsible for your pleasure.

By doing this you create separation. Rather than accepting their state in that moment as it was, or embracing their unique way of feeling, receiving or being in pleasure you had your own agenda to get them off, make them feel a certain way. By doing so you made it all about you. (This happens outside the bedroom too: expecting another to laugh with us at our own joke is an example.)

Choosing to own our pleasure instead of placing our expectations of pleasure on someone else opens the doorway to knowing ourself to greater depths. It also opens the doorway to really knowing and understanding another as you witness their unique ways of feeling and exploring pleasure.

My client Jim sat with me recently as we were discussing his strong passion for touch. He stated "When I am with a woman I want her to feel what I am feeling, and I believe this is part of my responsibility. I feel such a strong need to get her off."

What if she did not want to feel the same pleasure you felt? What if she did not desire for you to come to her with an agenda to please her because you thought it was in her best interest?

What if her desire was to witness your pleasure as your own unique pleasure? What if she desired to come to you wide open to share her unique pleasure and erotic nature as it naturally unfolded with you, without it being manipulated by your agenda?

Your partner's desire is to experience you, the depth and even unchartered territories of you. They are not wanting for you to think your job is to get them off or turn them on.

I offered him a different perspective. What if by putting down the agenda and idea of responsibility or performance he just showed up in his pleasure and allowed her to come to him in her natural timing; what if she were invited to show up in her unique pleasure? The natural flow that comes from that invitation would have the quality of receptivity to it, where she would want to merge and became present.

Now would that not feel more empowering for each and would there not be so much more to discover and share if sex is approached in such a way? The more in our own pleasure, in our own body we are, the more we actually feel these heightened states of arousal and pleasure.

Trust in this pleasure of yours! Trust that when your partner is ready, and naturally opens to their pleasure they will come to emerge more profoundly and deeply than you ever imagined.

# When Your Sexual Expectations Fail You

Oh those pesky expectations. They have a sneaky way of showing up in just about anything we do. Let us embrace our humanness, and accept that we will make expectations in relationships. It is part of our perfectly human experience, isn't it? The key, which you now hold, is to tap-in to your presence and awareness and identify when your own expectations start to overshadow the reality of the experience, and to see when another person's expectations of you are doing the same.

We have seen how expectation can come from outside: from societal pressures to perform or behave in a certain way, and from cultural conditioning and the awful way we were taught about sex. Expectation can come from within too. When expectation comes from within, as it so often does with sex, it is driven by desires, feelings and needs that have gone unmet and perhaps even unacknowledged.

Those unmet needs turn into expectations when we make those we are relating to responsible for fulfilling our desires and needs. When they fall short, it is natural for disappointment to set in.

Imagine you're on a date with your partner or lover. Your mind is racing with ideas of how you want the rest of the night to go, how you are going to be that wild, passionate man with an erection that stays rock hard all night and who has the most powerful ejaculation of a lifetime. But what if now that your mind is so busy, your parts just won't comply? In this moment your heart sinks, worry increases and you feel the stressful disconnection of heaviness taking over. Does this sound familiar?

I have worked with so many men with this issue. What I am finding is that these men have the same desire to be held, to be nurtured, to be embraced as we all do. They want the sex to be amazing, they want to touch the soul of their partners and feel the same in return. But somewhere along the way both men and women picked up a preconceived idea of what this means. That preconceived idea is so far from the truth.

The Manic Mind, which hides the depth of vulnerable intimacy you truly crave, takes over. That Manic Mind, with all its expectations, creates the symptoms of erectile dysfunction.

Women, the same desire for explosive sex and preconceived notions of what that means will have you thinking how you must achieve orgasm to really be a women. In the end, your Manic Mind become so disconnected from feeling what's happening in your body, your nervous system is holding on so tightly that nothing can come in the midst of all that contraction.

Some sexual expectations don't just get in the way in the moment, they can happen in longer term relationships too. Some of the more common sexual expectations I've seen in longer relationships are:

**Sexual desire** — Expecting you and your partner's sexual desire to be at the same degree all the time. It is common that those you are in relationship with will, at times, have a different degree of sexual desire than you. It is important to not take this personally. Remember, get clear with your feelings and have self-responsible communication about what each of you is feeling and needing. Co-create something that will assist in the meantime.

**Orgasm** — The need for you and your partner to orgasm or ejaculate during sex. So often sex is entered into with so much of an agenda. One of those agendas is that you are responsible for getting your partner off or to orgasm and if they don't there is something wrong.

**Sexual preferences don't change** — Guess what? They do. This idea will continue to create disconnection and suffering in your relating. People change, that means who you were when you met doesn't exist today. Get curious, ask questions, have regular check-in's or more to discuss what are your top turn-ons and sexual preferences. This will include touch, oral versus penetrative sex, kinks, how much foreplay is desired, positions and even the time of day.

When your sexual expectations fail you, you can get lost in an endless tunnel of blame and shame. We live in a culture where people are constantly turning to something outside themselves to fix what's wrong. They are too frightened to go inward. These fixes work like drugs: they keep the Manic Mind in control, the fear locked in and intimacy at bay.

What if you took one small step to turn this around? As an intimacy and relationship expert I have seen again and again that even a small step has a way of tricking the mind's tight fearful grip and letting the body feel safe for a moment. In that sacred moment there is an opportunity for a whole new pathway to open up.

I helped a client make that first small step just last week by asking a series of questions. I asked, "What if there were nothing to attain? What if there were no idea of what sex was supposed to look like, or sound like, or feel like? What if you're only intention was to be more present to what was happening in the moment?"

What if—by pausing, allowing in a couple of breaths, and focusing on what is happening inside your body—you could really deepen the pleasure and intimacy you feel?

When you get here, the need to attain an erection or have an orgasm to prove how much fun you're having, falls away. And you sink back into your joy, sharing intimacy, connection and pleasure in a different way.

## *Opening the Path*

This is how to take that first small step that changes everything. You may want to have a professional help you with this process.

1. Whether alone or with your partner, create a safe environment where you can be present and deeply listen to those old hidden parts of yourself with undivided attention. Be aware when you are caught up with a mind filled with expectations of yourself or another. Uncover the desires that lie underneath those expectations.

2. In the midst of sexual frustration, when things aren't working as you had wanted, pause, close your eyes, start to bring you awareness to your breath. Maybe put your hands on your lower belly or your genitals and say to yourself "I let go of goals and expectations. It is okay to relax and enjoy this moment. I am perfect as I am now."

3. When you are relaxed, observe your physical body and ask yourself "What do I find joyful in this moment? What feels good to me right now?" Be present and observe; your body will answer you physically. Often you will feel your body relax, you will feel certain pleasurable sensations in your body. If you're with a partner, you will feel that their presence and touch feel good on your skin.

4. Now you are present, you are able to enjoy this moment instead of being locked away in thinking it is supposed to be something else. When we think an experience has to be a certain way, we create separation between ourselves and the experience as it happens, and we miss out on the pleasure and intimacy that is there to be shared and felt. Keep your focus on the sensations of the moment.

5. If you're with a partner, you can begin to share what does feel good. "Let's caress each other, let's spoon and breath body to body, let's sit with one on top and the other in a chair Indian style, while naked, skin to skin. Let's play with soft penetration if that naturally follows." Be without a goal and inquire what feels pleasurable and what awakens intimacy.

Commit to putting down the attachment to the outcome, and rather inquiring what feels pleasurable and what awakens intimacy in the moment.

We are opening a new path. A path that leads away from disconnection and harm, from the fears and prohibitions our culture has laden upon us, away from our expectations of ourselves and our lovers, and towards a deeper, more soulful connection to our selves and our partners and to the moment. We are also opening the path to pleasure and fun, to sex that absolutely sizzles!

## Exploring Fantasy

When relationships thrive there is awareness, presence, play and fun. This is especially true in the bedroom! I'm talking about sexual fantasies, desire and quite possibly a bit of kink. People's opinions of what fun is vary as much as their desires do. When you find an emotionally stable, mature person where there is mutual consent to share a desire and common values, there are infinite possibilities for fun.

Now, things like kink or BDSM may or may not be for you. Your desires may be as simple as wanting to be touched in a specific way, but you have been scared to be touched that way, or even ask for it. Regardless, I encourage you to keep an open heart while reading. You don't need to be into kink to understand the importance of mutual care, love, presence, boundaries, and yes, consent.

Where to Start? You move as fast as the slowest link. You progress as fast as the slowest person is able. You learn to understand each other, make choices, teach each other. This work builds trust and helps you gain emotional clarity.

Start by being self-responsible and geting really clear on what your own desires and needs surrounding those desires are. This is where you use all those skills you developed by building your relationship with yourself.

Use your Deep Listening and communication skills so that you and your partner can communicate your fantasies without the fear of being rejected, and so that it feels safe to say no without fear of losing something. Empowering each other to make clear decisions based on your needs and desires is a real intimacy booster.

Some of my clients enjoy their BDSM play. They create a healthy empowered playing field beginning with talking. They both set boundaries, discuss fantasies, needs, and safe words. For when things get to be too much, they know and understand beforehand what signals are used when someone needs to pause. The realm of fantasy (whatever it may be for you) is explored to fulfill curiosity about each other. It is intimacy building.

What is so beautiful about discussions like these is that they not only build intimacy, but they create freedom and liberation. People are able to own their sexuality. They no longer have to fear what they desire because all of those feelings that come from other people judging—shame, guilt, embarrassment—are swept away with good communication and understanding.

You may want your fantasy to remain purely imaginary, or you may want a part or all of it to come true. Sometimes fantasy remains fantasy because it is just not possible to make it real due to some safety concern or simply because it is so imaginary that it just isn't accessible.

Let's have some fun and look at some fantasies now...

### *The delivery man fantasy.*

Imagine you are in the kitchen preparing dinner and you hear a knock at the door. You open the door surprised to see a delivery many with a special package for you.

Without a word, he comes in really close to you, wraps his arms around your waist, pulling you tightly in so you feel the heat of his body penetrate into you. You giggle a bit, a little nervous, part of you knows you are in the middle of cooking dinner, yet you start to feel your thighs quivering and lips moisten. You shyly start to pull away but come back melting farther into his strong embrace.

He is concerned for your dinner prep so he takes you to the kitchen to assist in making that delicious meal. "Let me help you with that," he says as he gathers the edges of your blouse in his fists before he tears it off you. "The temperature seems to be getting quite hot." And he feels your sweat dripping down your thighs as he grazes his hands softly up your skin.

He tells you to keep doing what you were doing as he slowly starts to undo your skirt. He allows his tongue to make its way up between those juicy thighs...

Have you ever had a deliver man or woman fantasy?

There are so many ways to create fantasies and so many ways to explore your undiscovered desires. The possibilities range from being ravished, to surrender, to passion with a stranger such as the kitchen scene, to having a full tie-me-up-and-spank-me scene with your lover or partner. How about lunch time sex on the patio?

Having sex outside of the bedroom adds an element of excitement for many. Society teaches us that sex is for behind closed doors and that we don't talk about it in public. Well I say sex is best outside of the bedroom especially if you have a multiple room house. Part of the excitement is going against the norm. There may be some mild exhibitionist in you, or having the thought "what if someone sees us?" can be arousing. How about getting bent over the kitchen table or fucked in the shower?

Let's look at a very short set of examples of sexual fantasies.

**Playing the Dom** — Being the dominate lead in your sexual exploration with your partner. Maybe you desire to play that Dom side and have your lover do what you wish and be at your beck and call.

**Threesome** — Have you met someone and thought "I wonder how it would be to have them in bed with my partner and I?" Or if you are single, maybe you have a desire to explore sex with more than one person at the same time.

**Center of attention** — How about being watched and witnessed by others? They may not be sexually engaging with you, but you and your love, in the midst of your passion are being celebrated and adored by onlookers from around the room.

**Being dominated** — Being told what to do. Does it turn you on to have your partner tell you what and how to do it to them? Do you like to be dominated and ravished? Do you want to be tied up, spanked and forced into surrender?

**Sex with the same sex** — Maybe you have yet to sexually or sensually engage with the same gender yet you daydream of another woman orally pleasing you, or kissing you. I have talked to many men who are heterosexual and have a fantasy or have thought about what it might be like if another man gave them oral sex.

**Voyeurism** — Watching others when they are naked or engaged in sexual activity.

Now as I mentioned sometimes fantasies are just that, fantasies. The turn on comes from imagining the experience and you may not desire to actually make the fantasy real. Sometimes it is more exciting to just think about it. Every phase of sharing fantasies is a very intimate experience. You may go through all the phases or only one.

*Steps to Sharing Your Fantasies*

Let's take a closer look at some of the steps or phases you will go through in building a sharing a fantasy with a partner or more! Remember to go at the pace of the slowest link, and that you're not obligated to develop a fantasy any further than you feel good about.

1. Self discovery. Reflect and make a list in your journey of some of your sexual likes, desires, fantasies even the ones you think are quirky… especially the ones you think are quirky.
2. Set up a time to share fantasies and desires. I love creating sacred space to do this in. This means people are choosing to show up present, compassionately and want to listen deeply and engage in the conversation.
3. Take turns sharing. I like the idea of one person sharing their top three and choosing which one to go more into in step by step description. Just describing the fantasy or desire becomes like foreplay and can be so activating.
4. Keep breathing, pay attention the whole time to how your body is feeling; share what comes up for you. Such as "I feel a bit nervous and embarrassed in sharing this," and then keep sharing.

5. Do you want to create a scene? This would be the moment to go deeper into what the experience would look like, which fantasy you want to create together. You want to go into the very specifics of it so when the time comes to play it out, you can simply relax into it and enjoy the playtime together with nothing to think about.

If you get as far as creating a scene with your partner, you will want to plan out these details: what props or items does the scene need? Candles, ropes, handcuffs, specific bedsheets, oils, lube, condoms, flogger, special sexy outfits, shoes, kitchen apron, etc.

What are the logistics? What location, house, room, garden etc. will the scene take place in? Will you need to be picked up? Will it be a secret hideaway? Will you need to arrange for a babysitter? Or an extended lunch break?

Do you need a safe-word? In acting out any fantasy you need to be able to communicate if you need to pause, or something does not feel right, or you are emotionally triggered. In scenes with any kind of dominance play, you create safe-words, and prior to the scene, you always get clear consent. A safe word is a word you would not ordinarily utter in a sexual situation, it is meant to stand out as separate from the fantasy playing out. I like simple words like "red light" to stop everything, "yellow light" to drop the intensity and invite in more presence. Whatever you choose, make sure its meaning is clear and that you have a way to stop the play.

Now it's your turn, fantasies and sexual desires come in all sorts of packag

es.

## Sex Beyond Penetration

I want to put one of the most pervasive and persistent expectations to rest: the expectation that sex means penetration. Sometimes penetrative sex may not be the right fit for your experience, or seeing as you've just read the section on exploring fantasy, perhaps you want to explore new routes of pleasure and sexual expression.

Here are some ideas for sex beyond penetration. But don't let this list limit your expression.

**Self pleasure together** — Watching a lover or partner self pleasure is such an erotic delight to indulge in. It is simply hot and you might dive right in and enjoy your own self pleasure while watching. This does not have to be done in the same place or same country. Skype or Zoom are both great for some sexy cyber moments of self pleasuring and witnessing each other's arousal. This is a gift because it encourages you to stay in your own pleasure and allows the other to be in their pleasure simply to be enjoyed by watching; no agenda other than to witness. That is super sexy in itself. If you are choosing to self pleasure over distance be prepared that afterwards you are not near your lover to cuddle and spoon up the sweetness. If you know this is a need of yours remember to check in before saying yes to this option, or have a friend or teddy bear near by to snuggle up with. The other option is to set up the scene to have 15 minutes of sweet talk and gentle time together on Skype afterward and be clear on what that would involve.

**Oral sex** — Play the oral sex adventure, and maybe you want to test out some new moves. The art of going down on your lover and worshiping their yoni (vagina) or lingum (penis) adds a new element of passion and wild abandon and is a great way to practice fully surrendering as the receiver. You might even set up a play date that it is more interactive, where one of

185

you is the giver of oral sex the other is sharing what they like and what feels better or what direction to go. Learning while pleasuring adds a bonus to the fun and intimate connection.

Learn your body and another's body beyond penetration — there is so much more to activating pleasure than touching the genitals. Explore the erogenous zones on the body, tease your partner (sometimes less is more), build up the turn-on rather than overstimulating and coming quickly. Enjoy the journey of it, there is so much to explore and find pleasure in.

## Bring Back the Sizzle

The scorching flames of new passion have begun to wane, and your sex life now seems a little… mundane. Sound familiar? I have one word for you: foreplay! I believe the key to keeping sex hot in a long term relationship is to frequently engage in foreplay. Foreplay isn't limited to cuddling or sexual activity in the bedroom. Think of it as a way of collaborating with yourself and your partner. Use your inner fire to stoke that foreplay.

We spoke about tending to your own inner fire previously in the book. This is your wellspring which you and only you are responsible for filling. If you forget about this well, and constantly search outside of yourself for fulfillment and fuel, your wellspring will dry up. This will end up leaching into your relationship and draining all which remains of everyone's well.

You want your relationship to feel like a vast ocean of abundant energy. You want to feel vital, alive, and joyful when you are with those you love. Remember self-sourcing is your number one go-to. When you are doing what you love, living your passion, and living your unique genius, this is attractive. It is part of tending to your sacred inner fire. I want to remind you of two keys to keeping that inner fire burning.

1. Remember what you love to do as an independent person out side of your relationship and without your lover or partner. Do you enjoy art, playing music, hiking, dancing, sports or meditation? Do it.
2. Self Pleasure. Touching yourself and knowing your body and pleasure is a huge fire builder for when you come together to share your turn-on with your beloved.

Foreplay outside of the bedroom is equally as important as it is inside, play being a key factor in your relationship to yourself and your lover. Make time for fun, silliness, joy, and laughter. You know... like you did in the beginning!

Maybe it's a sexy whisper in your lover's ear as you're watching a movie on the sofa. How about sending an unexpected text message to your partner telling them how you plan to pleasure them when they come home?

Flirtatiously brushing your body against your lover's body while reaching for the refrigerator door can set the tone for the day. Run your hands over your partner's bum or genitals as if it were an accident as you head out the door for work. While hiking together, suddenly stop as if something caught your eye and boldly pull your partner in close for a brief, ravishing kiss before proceeding nonchalantly. When you're standing in the checkout line at the grocery store, turn toward your lover and share a lingering, loving gaze and a sweet smile.

I once gave a client of mine, Adam, a sexting homework assignment, as he was working on confidence and comfort expressing his sexuality and desires. For months there was a lot of resistance as he worked through thoughts of shame, embarrassment, and fear of what his partner might think. Finally, he completed the assignment and was more than happy to share his experience with me. His nerves morphed into excitement and empowerment when his wife, who was at a work conference, was thrilled by his erotic, flirtatious email and told him he had made her day!

How often do you take the time to appreciate and spice up the rushed moments of life out of the bedroom? The few minutes of shared time in the kitchen before dashing off to work or or to shop for groceries is the place you can find that spark that restarts a raging fire.

*Practice Autonomy*

It's easy to get derailed from your solo time when the excitement of your relationship and the joy found in your bond is so profound. Chances are the aspects that attracted you and your partner to each other initially were your autonomous natures. You were both living your lives independently fueled by your own passions and desires.

A few nights ago, I came home to my lover after a week long getaway to focus on writing. I had just received a proof of the book cover from my graphic designer and I was so amped. I had the excitement of a child, and could not stop talking about it! As I showed off the design to my lover, he suddenly grabbed me, and literally swept me off my feet, into a sexual adventure. Seeing my turn-on (my book project) was a real turn-on for my lover, which lead to unencumbered sex followed by a grounding meditation.

Another example of maintaining your autonomy might be to sleep in separate rooms one night a week. Treat yourself to a special date night with you! Light some candles, draw a bath, dance alone, set the stage for some self-pleasuring and fall asleep to the sound of your own heartbeat. Practice turning yourself on and returning to your lover or partner with new found passion.

# Intimacy Outside the Bedroom

Intimacy allows us to feel deeply, to awaken all the senses and acknowledge in some way an interconnection with the people and environment around us. It allows us to feel as if we are permeating the existence of all things. It feels like a deep knowing, and being known.

What would the world be like if all experiences were entered with this deep penetrating knowing? Why would this penetrating quality be thought of as only physical, sexual penetration? Intimacy is not a dirty word. A lifetime of conditioning has left us with a dysfunctional interpretation of how intimacy applies to all our relationships. It is a myth that intimacy and sex are the same thing.

You have a level of intimacy with your children, parents, family, friends, colleagues, grocer, as well as your lover or spouse. Of course, all of these unique expressions vary in the depth of intimacy shared. However, the depth of intimacy you share is only limited by how much you feel safe and comfortable with allowing another to see and know you.

My client Ron realized that he was a genius at putting on an image or playing a particular role so others would accept him both personally and in business. Have you ever had one of those moments where you would play a part and act the way you felt others wanted you to or expected you to? Well, Ron knew how to make the sale, how to win the right people over, but realized in the midst of all of that, he had forgotten who he really was. Ron had used his ability to put on a disarming mask so often that intimacy was becoming a distant dream.

These masks created a barrier to accessing real connection. You might ask "isn't this is a good way to hide and protect yourself?" Sometimes life shows us that it isn't safe to just share our unique truth or how we truly feel in each moment. And by doing so we have co-created high levels of disconnection in the world. How often as humans do we do this, take on the a role so it is acceptable by society, community, relationships?

Unfortunately it has become the norm and the disconnection and detachment that results is the reason we see so much strife and fighting in the world. How can anyone truly care about or care for another if they cannot allow another to know them?

As an entrepreneur and transformational leader, I find ways to share my stories when I'm speaking and teaching, along with how I apply the tools and techniques in this book to my real life. You have witnessed some of that already. This naturally opens up a door to a closer relationship with those I am working and engaging with and also creates a sense of safety.

To open intimately we want to be clear on our own boundaries so we may be aware of another's boundaries. Remember boundaries are guidelines to be aware of that inform ourselves and another about how closely we might interact. Is it okay to touch, is there a particular distance between each other, how much time do you have for this meeting? These are all kinds of boundaries. When we know these guidelines we can approach the experience full-on while honoring each other in the moment.

When you know someone can relate to you, doesn't it feel safer or easier to get vulnerable? These are all qualities that come out when we open that intimate door.

## *Getting Intimate with the Inanimate*

The benefits of increased intimacy extend and extend and extend. They go so far beyond relating to any one person. I had a client, Andy, who was a phenomenal surfer. At this stage in his life he had traveled the world for 30 years surfing the biggest waves. When he reached out to me he expressed a desire to become a better lover. He found himself projecting into the future, and even had a checklist when he dated people. Andy was so caught up in his head analyzing the situation that he lacked presence, awareness, sensitivity, emotional availability and he was downright scared to be vulnerable. This means he lacked that quality of intimacy we are speaking of.

During our work together Andy realized he needed to focus less on finding the one true partner, and more on the one inside of himself. This meant that everyone he met was in some way the one when he was with them. Why? Because Andy was so present and available for people now. Each meeting holds a message for us, an invaluable intimate exchange between humans. When this became Andy's reality, people instantly trusted him and wanted to share vulnerability and conversation. Strangers he would meet on the beach out in his day just naturally opened up to him, and after 30 years of being the top, his surfing skills increased 10 fold. Surfers have a relationship to the surfboard, to the waves and to the other surfers. It takes a deep level of presence, awareness, sensitivity, and reverence for the water.

He deepened his intimate connection with the board and the water because he opened up more inside of himself. He could read the waves, know his next move and became more at one with the water, like the water was permeating him. The interconnection between him and the water became clear. This is intimacy.

## Non-Sexual Touch

What are the ways you have experienced touch and human contact in your life? Everyday forms of touch can bring us emotional balance and better health. There are so many ways—everyday, incidental gestures that we usually overlook—that we share touch. And though you may take some of those ways for granted, they have a profound effect on the human connection we share.

Here is a short list of ways we touch each other during the day that we might not think of as intimacy building, but in fact are.

- Holding a parent's or grandparent's hand,
- Sharing a hug with a friend,
- Shaking someone's hand,
- Wrapping your arms around someone to comfort them or be comforted,
- Gently placing a hand on the knee to comfort,
- Receiving or giving a massage,
- Cuddling,
- Rocking or holding a baby,
- Sportsmanship contact such as patting on the back.

All these incidental forms of touch are an unspoken language and a means for connection and sharing compassion. The latest research suggests that touch is a fundamental component to human communication, and emotional and physical health.

For example, one experiment looked at the effect of touch on premature infants. A group of premature infants that received body stroking and passive movement of the limbs developed appreciably faster than their counterparts who did not receive the touch. They gained weight 47% faster, they were more active and alert, and they had significantly shorter hospital stays[7].

Our skin is our largest organ and a great doorway for information to pass via touch. There is a series of cells in your skin called Merkel cells, which, in the words of the scientists who study them "actively tune mechanosensory responses[8]." That is to say, they actively feed data about touch from your skin straight to your nervous system. The body responds physiologically with a surge of hormones, and if the touch is caring and connective as in some of the examples above, you'll likely get an increase of oxytocin which was coined the "cuddle hormone[9]."

Jeanne AbateMarco, the clinical nurse coordinator of the Department of Integrative Health Programs at NYU Langone Medical Center says that touch is "integral to the human experience." I agree.

## Hugging

Let's zero in on just one of those everyday forms of contact: hugging. I absolutely value the moments that remind me how much I love hugging! Especially when two people have the

[7] Field TM, Schanberg SM, Scafidi F, Bauer CR, Vega-Lahr N, Garcia R, Nystrom J, Kuhn CM, "Tactile/kinesthetic stimulation effects on preterm neonates," *Pediatrics* 77(5) (1986 May): 654-8. https://www.ncbi.nlm.nih.gov/pubmed/3754633

[8] Srdjan Maksimovic, Masashi Nakatani, Yoshichika Baba, Aislyn M. Nelson, Kara L. Marshall, Scott A. Wellnitz, "Epidermal Merkel cells are mechanosensory cells that tune mammalian touch receptors," *Nature* 509 (29 May 2014): 617–21. doi:10.1038/nature13250

[9] K. Aleisha Fetters, "You Feel Me? The Science Of Being Touched (& Why It's So Good For You)," *Refinery29.com*, October 19, 2014, http://www.refinery29.com/human-touch-benefit, accessed September 2017

ability to just be in the hug, breath together, be still together, laugh and drop into an open heart. Sharing a hug seems so simple, yet, for many, hugging is downright scary.

I want to share a story with you. I was out walking with a new friend one day. We had met each other through community and this particular walk was the first time we shared some quality time together in conversation, just the two of us. We walked and talked for an hour and I realized how much I really just wanted to be touched. We walked brushing arms from time to time, arms wrapped around each other with great ease, and when it came time for a hug to close our date it was so liberating to say, very loudly, I might add, "Oh my god, that felt so good!"

Being on the road, away from loved ones, I realized that my body and heart really missed the nurturing of loving touch. We both laughed and I asked for another and another and another. I think we shared five long hugs, breathing together, laughing and allowing the softness of the heart to blossom in me.

Now I am a very open, hugging kind of person by nature. I thought about how so many people want to share this kind of closeness. They want it yet do not feel comfortable asking for it, do not have the space, the emotional clarity to feel safe. Nor do they have boundary skills to ask for what they need. When you are aware of your personal boundaries in a situation you are able to navigate what you clearly want and don't want. You are also able to understand what is okay to ask for based on another person's boundaries.

Imagine for a moment a world where everyone felt so safe in their connection to their own body and values, so secure in their sexuality, that hugging no longer felt like a threat. You let go of the belief that hugging means you are going to have sex with the other person and intimacy is welcomed in.

Think of how often you have hugged without truly sinking into it: maybe you held your breath the entire time; or what about the old stick-the-butt-out hug as if you're trying not to catch cooties; oh and don't forget that good old side-hug, back-pat kind of thing.

I believe we have all felt the benefits of receiving a hug. For many hugging is an extremely effective way to shift loneliness, sickness, depression, anxiety and stress because of the touch factor, feeling connection and love. A deep, connective, long hug where hearts are pressing together has a way of creating a sense of support and nurturing. Hugs are able to increase levels of oxytocin in the body which can shift feelings of anger and isolation. Those really long embraces, the ones where you really allow yourself to melt and breathe for a minute, elevates the mood and serotonin levels in the body.

On a deep emotional level hugs ask us to let our guard down, be present, open, vulnerable and in the heart. They take us out of our chronic thinking patterns. You know the ones that keep us in control and far out of a surrendered heart. When you hug in such ways it takes us right into intimacy. You can no longer hide behind the personas, the masks, the armor that have been built through a lifetime of stories and conditioning.

## Intimacy Friction in the Workplace

How well do you know your colleagues? Do you share short lived, superficial conversations which have very little attention given to them? Unfortunately you don't always get to choose the people you work with. In this beautiful world of being perfectly human we all have emotional past stories and different personalities that come with us into the workplace. And those stories can make friction between colleagues.

Friction between personalities in the work place can lower productivity, leaving employees unhappy and less motivated. Friction and disagreement can get in the way of a team developing bonds.

It's a tricky problem to solve because the people involved are not motivated in their interacting with each other by the desire to get to know each other and form a bond; they're there to get a job done. How do you deal with friction if there is not already an intimate bond where you feel you can openly communicate your needs or feelings?

My client Melanie was miserable at work day in and day out. She felt unseen, unheard and even undervalued by her boss. These feelings were real for Melanie, her conditioned story and Manic Mind had her believing she was worthless, that her voice did not matter, that others created her value and that they were to blame for this situation. You may relate and this can be a slippery slope for sure.

The reality of having an intense disagreement is that you cannot change how the other person is acting or how they are perceiving or experiencing the disagreement. We are not responsible to change someone else (it is ill advised to try) but we do all have the ability to shift ourselves from within. When we do this, often what naturally follows are changes outside of us. The self-responsible aspect of handling friction at work means the change has to start within us.

Melanie began to work with me to address the way she experienced her worth and what her story was telling her. How to change it? For Melanie it was a step by step process of uncovering, understanding and owning her own feelings and needs, clearing her emotional suppressions at the root, developing her emotional intelligence so as to have more compassion for her colleagues, and master her communication formulas.

As she incorporated these changes she started to feel more confident from the inside no matter what happened with her boss or colleagues. As her confidence and her capacity to have compassion for her colleagues grew, she no longer felt she needed to protect herself. One day there was a debate building in the work place. The old Melanie would have kept her mouth quite, built up so much tension and frustration in her body and felt belittled and worthless. She realized she was the one belittling herself, no one else was doing this. In this certain case she decided to apply her emotional intelligence tools and communicate. She began by acknowledging what others were saying, and went on to share her opinion in a way that was not putting their opinions down, from there she stayed open and curious.

Melanie took responsibility to build new work relationships and a new platform for herself with her colleagues. She felt so much joy, exhalation and confidence, it spilled over into how others treated her at work. The quality of our relationship with others stems from the quality of our relationship with our own selves.

## Extending Intimacy to All Relationships

I believe that the root of many of the world's seemingly intractable problems is a lack of intimate connection. Many of the ills we see happening in the world are caused by people in the midst of survival, believing they are in this for themselves, alone, misunderstood and stuck in a cycle where they have stuffed down the pain and feel gagged, unable to let it out.

You may think that struggling or fighting for what you want is going to get you the connection you desire. The point of this book is to show you that there is another way, one that is kinder, gentler to your whole being, one that takes into account the ecosystems around us and looks at our life from more of a holistic nature. That gentler way calls us to extend a sense of intimacy to all our relationships. We build understanding and we build trust.

As a final thought in this chapter, I want to give you some small tips that help build intimacy right off the bat. Incorporate these little actions into your interactions during the day and you will notice the world turns with a little more ease.

- Enter into your experiences with more presence.
- Slow down and breathe before engaging in the conversation or meeting.
- Keep eye contact, breathe during the conversation.
- Be curious and ask questions. It feels good to feel someone else is interested. It builds empathy.
- When you're shaking hands, pause during the hand shake, look into the eyes, breathe. I even enjoy cupping the other person's hand, shaking with one and laying my other loosely over it.
- Make use of your compassionate communication skills and acknowledge what others are sharing. If you feel differently, acknowledge it, and afterwards, share your view in a way that does not demand they agree.

So the next time you are interacting with another person pay attention to how relaxed and authentic you are in your communication, are you curious and asking questions and really deeply listening to the answers? Are you animated, open, relaxed in sharing with this person when they ask you questions? Check in to see how you body is responding to your environment. Is it tight and tense or open to feel life? Get intimate with life and watch greater ease, vitality and wellbeing follow.

# Sharing the Breath

Life begins with breath and as you first opened these pages the breath was introduced as a vehicle to access greater awareness, presence, peace and clarity. Engaging with the breath is your means to feeling vitality just as constricting your breath is your pathway to misery and confusion. Your breathing has the potential to grow into the most intimate experience you will feel. Wouldn't it be an ideal thing to share with another?

It may not be obvious that your daily breathing practice has already been having an effect on the quality of your life and relationships, but it has. When you get spooked or panicked and the body goes into fight or flight or freeze mode the breath starts to physiologically change. This change in breath echoes the panic in the brain and you have learned you can either get lost in that misery and panic or you can bring your awareness to your breathing and return it to a deep easy breathing pattern. This in turn calms the brain and helps you restore collectedness. So your breath is like taking medicine to alleviate the pain and suffering during a flare up. And done daily, it acts like preventative medicine. Wouldn't you prefer relating with others who are able to communicate with you in a calm, collected manner?

Your breath also has the power to be preventative medicine. Your daily breathing practice naturally creates a more harmonious, peaceful, vital state of body, mind and spirit. If you have been using the Audio Home Practice (available on my website, soulfulrelatinginstitute.com), or have received facilitated sessions, then you are really honing the means to integrate and clear past emotional suppressions. You are going deeper to remove the obstacles and triggers at their root. This would be a huge component of self responsibility and a gift to any form of personal or business relationship.

There is also a much more intimate component of the breath. When I feel my breath open and easily moving through my body, I feel like the breath is making love through me. I mean to say that the qualities that go with lovemaking show up in my breathing. It is nourishing, loving, caressing, increasing of life. It is touching you ever so gently, massaging the organs as it moves. Imagine for yourself, what feelings, or qualities are present in making love. I often say life itself is making love to me when I am radically aware of every moment and I feel things so deeply in my body.

Sharing that profoundly open state with another has limitless possibilities. Sharing breath works to deepen intimacy in a sexual or non-sexual way. I am going to outline four different scenarios in which you can share breathing to enhance the level of intimacy you enjoy.

- Ways to share the breath:
- In a dyad (meaning two people) with a platonic friend,
- In a dyad with a romantic partner,
- In a dyad with a sexual partner,
- In a small group of close friends.
- I suggest once you have completed your breathing experiences together, take turns sharing your experience by using a dyadic integration format which you will find below.

### The Romantic Partner or Platonic Friend Breathing (Non-Sexual)

Prepare a clean space or room by setting soft lighting, having near at hand water and whatever else you want to inspire a relaxed comfortable atmosphere. Reflect that you are sharing a soulful connection, supporting each other in relaxing the nervous system, and offering up presence for your friend or romantic partner through your breath. Remember the focus will be on open mouthed, full circular breathing as described in the beginning of the book. Open your mouth, think of the breath like a circle or a wave connecting the inhale and the exhale. Focus on an easy effortless inhale, and just let the breath go for the exhale, like a silent sigh. This is non-sexual and simply an intimate loving space you are both creating. Make sure to have discussed this prior so both of you are clear on the intentions of this share and clear on each other's boundaries. I will describe four different non-sexual ways to share breathing with a platonic friend or romantic partner.

**Sitting facing your partner** — Set a timer for 10 minutes in total. Place two backed chairs facing each other. You will want your back supported for this exercise because we intend to fully relax the diaphragm and back muscles. Sit with your knees just loosely touching the other's. If you're comfortable begin the breath with eyes open, you will find that one of you may have a more open breath and that simply by hearing and feeling the other will be supported. Breathe with eyes open for about a minute or two. After that, close your eyes and continue this circular dynamic breathing. Both of you start to go on your shared individual journey for the next five minutes. Remember attending to the self is a gift to nurture any platonic or romantic relationship. After about five minutes, continue to breath while you open your eyes for another minute to connect back in again. Be gentle with yourself and open your eyes slowly as you have just created a heightened state and may be more sensitive to your environment. After a minute close your eyes again, slow the breath down, take a few deep breaths in, letting the exhale happen with a sigh. Enjoy the stillness and quiet together before rushing back to talk.

**Sitting back to back** — Find a comfortable position that you may sit back to back leaning into one another. Your back will be fully touching with equal weight distributed between you. Depending on your flexibility or restrictions you may need props such as pillows and cushions. It will be important you both feel comfortable and are able to relax. If you can't get comfortable back-to-back, don't worry and choose one of the other non-sexual shared breathing experiences. One is not any better than the other, they are simply different experiences.

Once you have the props and cushions you require, and you are sitting comfortably with your backs against each other, position your legs either outstretched or crossed. Place your hands on your lower belly, and with an open mouth, begin to allow your breath to find that wave-like rhythm. Don't force it but allow it to start small or shallow if it wishes. As you slow down and relax, your breathing will open and grow in volume. Begin to feel the movement of your spine and your partner's spine as the breath circulates, let the torso be relaxed and moved by the breath.

**Spooning** — Anyone can spoon, remember it is not only for romantic partnership. The benefits of cuddling are endless, just Google it and you will find all the health benefits of conscious touch, cuddling, and hugging all over the web today. Spooning is a very intimate exchange and you should only engage in it with a platonic or romantic partner with whom you feel comfortable and safe enough to share such a vulnerable experience. Remember to have that boundary discussion, and set personal intentions for this experience before beginning. Having this clear to begin with will set the tone for relaxing into an enjoyable intimate exploration of your breath and vulnerability. Spooning itself I find calms the nervous system and lets one give up the idea that they need to do everything for themselves.

Prepare a room by creating a cozy floor space with cushions, blankets and pillows. You can do this in a backyard or cozy private outdoor setting. If you're doing it with more of a romantic partner, you may choose a bed, though you should create an agreement that this experience will be non-sexual. This will let the mind relax, stepping away from any agenda and helping you be present to yourself and the moment.

Start by gently bringing your awareness to the sensations of your body against the floor or bed. Feel the way it feels to be held or to lay in such a way. Notice what begins to happen in your body, physiologically. Don't attach any story to the sensation, but simply witness what the body feels as you continue. Bring you awareness to the natural breath, how your body, how your partner's body moves with the breath. Slowly begin the open-mouthed gentle wave-like breath. Allow the wave to increase in volume and become slightly more active (though this particular breathing experience will be gentler in nature than the others).

**Facing each other with legs outstretched over your partner's** — Also know as Yab Yum. For this breathing experience you will want to be sitting on the floor with a cushion or something to support your back. Choose which of you will have legs on bottom and which of you on top. Outstretch the legs like a wide "V", sitting with about one or two feet distance between your torsos. Rest your hands comfortably on each others waist to begin. Start your opened mouth, full circular breath from the lowest part of the belly upward. The wave-like breathing begins slowly in every experience. Here you start to sync up the breath. Alternate breathing with eyes open and closed. As with all these exercises, be present, feel what is happening in the body, feel the movement of the other. When you're both ready and feeling comfortable, you can adjust your position to sit in full Yab Yum. The partner on the bottom brings their legs into a cross legged position. The partner on top makes a high seat with about three couch pillows to prop their seat/pelvis higher. They wrap their legs around the other with about a foot or two distance between you. Place your hands on your parner's sacral area for support and continue circular breathing, belly to belly. The one on top can place their hands on the back of the heart and neck of their partner. Eventually let the body move and breath organically. Let the breathing happen for a set amount of time without reacting to what your body starts to feel. This is a beautiful precursor to deeper intimacy, so enjoy it.

### The Romantic or Sexual Partnered Breathing

Breathing is a tool to extend and deepen any sexual experience. During penetrative intercourse it can be used to prolong love making, assisting you in riding the waves of pleasure. And it can be used as a ceremonial means to close your lovemaking. As with the non-sexual breathing, I will describe a number of ways you can share.

**Facing each other with full penetration** — Laying down in your position of choice, upon first entering your partner or during a pause between highly aroused, wild moments of high sexual play, gently bring your awareness back to the breath, looking into each other's eyes all the while. If you are doing this exercise upon first penetration, begin to circulate your breath prior to penetration. Make sure that entering your partner is an invitation, don't assume and unconsciously penetrate without at first receiving that invitation. This is a special opportunity to honor each other's body and breath as sacred and for the gifts that they are. "May I enter you?" would be a great request.

Upon receiving a yes, continue to breathe, and slowing, have your penis (or strap-on, or whatever you're using) enter your partner. The breath increases your ability to feel, increasing your arousal and emotional connection. Invite whatever feelings arise to come in. I have cried many times during sexual intercourse and allowed the array of emotions to enhance the intimate experience shared with my partner. You will find your breath will organically awaken many feelings. Let your sexual lovemaking flow into all its many ways of expression together.

Breathe in the pauses. Often during the fiery passion it is easy to get caught up in the building phase of sex, the thrusting, the sweating, the quickening pace. The body starts to contract as we reach for that orgasm like we're straining to cross a finish line. The breath will be a great asset here to prolong the pleasure and sexual lovemaking time. When you notice you're short on breath, your sex has turned to mere physical movements (yes that may feel good but it can feel even better). Slow your movement down, pause with your foreheads touching, allowing your bodies to melt into each other. Breathe down through the belly into the genitals, all the way to the anus. Imagine the wave of breath from the anus up to the upper heart. Visualize that breath circulating through your whole torso connecting top to bottom, front to back. Visualize the same circle wrapping around both you and your partner. Allow this slower flow to open up to the next wave of wild abandon. This form of breathing may be used in most any position.

**Naked Yab Yum with possible soft penetration** — My favorite foreplay is to let the sexual experience naturally unfold. Let go of expectations of even the need to get an erection or be fully hard to enjoy this one. I know I love the pleasure of feeling a soft penis touching me and naturally, with every breath, getting harder while my yoni and all my sexual anatomy is slowly opening, pulsating, swelling in a desire to pull my partner into me. This is the natural magnetic attraction. Sit in Yab Yum like described previously in the non-sexual version. Here you will be fully naked, yoni (vagina) connected and touching to your partners penis. Possibly using your hand to gently guide the soft penis to touch the opening of your yoni. Depending on your genitals this may be achieved using a strap-on. Men, you can enjoy this with each other too, it will simply mean a few adjustments in positioning. Everything applies to all genders.

Draw your breath in through an open mouth, bringing it down through the belly, through the sexual center, to the anus, eventually allowing it to rise like a circle, from the anus, though the sexual center up to the upper chest. Sync your breath with your partner, allowing the arousal to build for at least ten minutes or more. If further penetration grows out of this and the desire is a full lovemaking experience, let this be like foreplay leading into the building waves of arousal.

**Post intercourse nose breathing** — Lay in any position, hold your partner and begin to inhale and exhale slowly through the nose. Slow your breathing down, allowing the inhale to last a full slow count of six seconds. Imagine pulling the breath up from the anus to the point between the eyebrows. Slowly push the breath down and out, back down to the anus and sexual center, for a count of six. Lay together focusing on this breath practice for roughly five minutes. If you desire longer, go for it! Otherwise come to resting together after breathing naturally for five minutes. This is a perfect way to ground your energy after penetrative sex.

*Group Breathing*

**In back-supported chairs set up in a circle** — A circle is a great way to build a connected experience. It not only allows everyone to easily see each other before and after the breath journey but it also creates an energetic seal. The circle becomes your so called forum. Once seated you may want to each speak your intention, what is something that you desire to manifest through this group breathing experience. Maybe more peace, an open heart, to feel more love, health or relaxation. Possibly there is a really big change in your life around which you would like to create more ease. Circles have a way of being very powerful, especially with a group of close friends. Once everyone has spoken close your eyes and place your hands on you lower belly. Allow in a belly breath with a sigh on the exhale three times. After that continue on to create the circular connected breath. In and out through the mouth, like a wave, allow the exhale to happen like a silent sigh.

Make sure you have set a timer, have either my guided audio breath journey or your favorite music playing so you don't have to think once you all begin. Choose anywhere from 5 to 30 minutes.

**Back to back in pairs** — This is one of my favorite ways to breath with someone. Whether a close friends or a lover. If you are pairing up with someone of a different height, make sure you have cushions to sit on so there is no strain in your back. Once positioned on the cushions sit with your back facing each other. Leaning gently against each other's back either cross legged if that is easy or with legs outstretched. Your backs want to be equal in weight against each other. Begin your circular connected breath and feel the rise and fall of the belly and spine. As you continue this style of breathing you will naturally begin to feel your torsos moving organically synchronized to each other's breath. Possibly even making circles or folding forward and back. Make sure not to force the movement. All you're doing is breathing and the breath and body easily find their rhythm. You choose how long you and your partner desire to do this. I enjoy starting slow, letting the energy and body build some fire and after quieting down again to a slow breath into stillness.

## Dyadic Integration

You can greatly enhance this shared breathing experience—or any shared experience for that matter—by using dyadic integration techniques. Dyadic integration is a formalized or formulaic way of listening to each other's share and experience. Deep Listening requires having no agenda of your own and not acting to fix your partner or approve what they are saying. How often when communicating do you feel anxious to get a word in, comparing their story to something you have experienced; or feel the urge to come up with a strategy to fix or help them? While you are doing all that, you are not really Deep Listening. One cannot be present or really listen if the mind is caught up in thinking or having an agenda.

Dyadic integration, when used in its full format in longer time frames, becomes soulful communication. As the two continue to share, what is shared may loose logic or common sense and begin to come from a deeper part of you. You may begin to share things never shared, or things that you had forgotten about. It is like peeling back thick layers and revealing what has not been seen or felt in a while. This also means it may feel uncomfortable, especially if it is a new experience for you. You may be awkward, and know that it's okay to feel awkward. The key is to observe—to the best of your ability, and without judgment—what you are feeling.

1. Choose how long you want to do this, and set a timer. Have the timer set for intervals as each one of you will share for an agreed time. For example, you may want to share in three minute intervals, with each of you having three opportunities to share. That will take a total of 18 minutes. Some gym timers let you set an interval time and the total number of intervals. If you're using a regular timer, set it for the interval length, and keep count of the number of shares you each have done. One of you will listen and the other will share.

2. A round of sharing is started when the listener inquires, "Tell me something you would like me to know." The speaker shares for the full interval.

3. The listener sits still and listens. They are not to nod their head, touch their partner, or make any comments no matter how much they desire. Your role as the listener is simply to sit still, be present with an open heart, breathe, and listen. The one talking shares what ever comes to them. It may not make sense, there does not have to be order or logic to what you are sharing. Remember to pause and breathe in the belly and talk slowly. Allow it to flow with a relaxed nervous system, stay feeling the sensations in the body, stay present. If words are difficult, pause and breath with your eyes open.

4. Once the timer indicates the interval is up, The listener says "thank you," and the roles change immediately without talking. The new listener makes the inquiry.

5. You go back and forth for all the rounds you agreed to. Once the full time is over you may agree to discuss anything that came up from this dyadic process more fully if you both desire.

# Relationships Evolve — Conscious Uncoupling

Developing a relationship is an opportunity to learn more about yourself and to grow as an individual. You learn so much from your partner directly and by working with them to make your relationship blossom like a wild garden, with no fences, yet with exquisite flowers, trees and luscious fruits. Building a relationship is a deep inviting thing that necessarily brings about change in your life. And somehow we have ended up with the idea that a relationship doesn't change, that it gets formed and then simply remains that way.

Who made up the rules that relationships are supposed to last forever, stay exactly as they were from the day you met someone? This is an idea that likely sprung up out of fear of change, fear of being out of control, fear of the unknown. We are conditioned to think relationships have to last forever, even if the spirit of the relationship is shifting or wanting to evolve. Our emotional needs become so lost in the desire to have the one-and-only with us forever. We hold on so tightly to our happily-ever-after.

The biggest disruption I find in any relationship is when you think you or your partner will be the same tomorrow as you are today. The entity of relationship is fluid. Love is fluid. When you're able to become fluid with the relationship this is where the nourishment and life thrive. Otherwise suffocation and pain happen, resentment sets in.

For a relationship to be truly empowering for all, it means honoring the seasons of change when they come. We change on a daily basis. What's more, the degree and the speed of those changes, also changes. There are ebbs and flows, there are storms and calm seas. That is the strength and the wisdom of a relationship.

This means the human needs and values that existed at the beginning of a relationship may be different months or years down the road. It is important to understand this and check-in regularly and to be radically honest with each other every day.

Relationships are an entity of their own. Even within a pair bonded relationship you actually have three bodies of intelligence. Yours, your partner's and the relationship itself. A relationship is something that is cultivated, like raising a child. It has its own energy which weaves together the individual truth of each person within the relationship and the relationship itself has a truth of its own. As you change and grow, so will the truth of the relationship.

We often enter relationships from a place of me and you. It is a place that has agendas, wanting to get something from the other. As a relationship gets older and more authentic in this stage of what I would call mature love, there is a shift from "how is this person or experience serving me?" to "how does this situation or choice serve the whole relationship?"

The relationship and the daily love shared takes on more of a calming, meditative quality that is so distinct from the electric new relationship energy. It thrives on inner quiet, awareness, self sourcing, presence and your emotional intelligence.

Relationships change in all kinds of ways. When they transition quickly or come to an end, it will, without a doubt, trigger some very deep, old relationship beliefs, and it will open old wounds. Resistance and non-acceptance are common. Playing the victim might be intoxicating for a while, blaming the other, questioning "how could they?" But the way forward is to make the transition happen with your partner in a conscious way.

Consciously transitioning a relationship may be a slow process requiring many months. It must happen gradually and organically because what takes place is as individual and unique as the relationship itself. The longer you are in relationship the longer the conscious transitioning typically takes. What goes into this from day to day is also personal choice and must reflect the unique needs of the individuals. I suggest taking from the processes and exercises in this chapter to assist you in finding a new balance that meets your needs. Although, you will have to tailor any processes to your situation.

## *My Personal Journey with Conscious Uncoupling*

Six days before my 45th birthday my beloved and I had a counseling session with a dear friend and mentor. We knew that this session was going to change our lives forever. We were there to make a conclusion out of the homework we had been doing for the previous two weeks.

We had spent those two weeks going deeper into our personal truths, getting to know our present day needs and feelings. We took time for self inquiry and journaling to really get clear on present day values and where our spirits or lives were calling us. We wanted to gain clarity on if we were aligned for our relationship to go deeper into our primary partnership or if it would swing the other direction into rich companionship and friendship. You can imagine that this work stirred up a lot of emotion for both of us.

As relationships evolve it is important to ask what is in the highest good for the relationship which is different from our in-the-moment emotional triggers or wants. Think about it. If a relationship is ending sometimes feelings of abandonment get triggered. When abandonment is triggered all that can be seen is how much one wants to cling to the other person for security and latch on to this shared experience. Even if in a bigger picture the two individuals have outgrown this shared experience of relating. You with me? It can be tough to understand in a world so focused on the I or me.

When it comes to mindful relating it is always about what is in the greatest alignment with the highest truth. Where is the integrity at? Now having said that, I can tell you that it is not always an easy path to forge. I look at my own internal fight and I have to laugh at it: my conversations with spirit, my own ebb and flow of peace and resistance.

My desires were to deepen our primary connection, that he come forward, ready to take that next step to meet me and my needs. So when I was thinking everything was finally shifting, my beloved realized he just was not there yet. Even though I felt such sadness and hurt I also felt he was truly honoring his truth and doing so in a way that was ultimately honoring me and our love. It was he who spoke the word "transitioning."

The relationship and myself received such a gift sharing this experience, this transition with a partner who offered so much presence to the relationship. So much that we formally took a year and slowly shifted how much we interacted and shared. Today I have left San Diego where we lived so I may follow my higher calling yet we still text nearly every day and talk at least once a week.

You may ask, how do I consciously transition a relationship if my partner or even a friend aren't that present, they're stuck in emotional trigger and unavailable. Remember any kind relationship may transition whether it is friendly, romantic or professional. All this means is the way you relate changes but doesn't always end. When another is not available, this is your time to step into radical self responsibility. Your sole responsibility is yourself. It would be your turn to take space, get clear on what serves your entire body, mind and spirit to thrive. What are your present day values and bottom lines in any relationship? This would be great to journal about, breathe and take solo time. All the processes in this book will be beneficial at this point.

When you get clear and are building your emotional intelligence muscle, you have the courage to shift the relationship direction using a proactive choice instead of running away in blame and anger.

I know that relationship transitions may not be easy. I know because my transition did not feel easy when I was in my mourning phase. My personal mourning started out intense. I was in extreme resistance to the transition. I resisted because I saw the bigger picture of the love we shared, even though I saw that my truth and his truth were in two different places.

I felt at the time I did not have a choice in all of this, that transitioning was ripping something out of my life—it felt unfair. My thing was wanting to have a choice. However the more I reflected on this transformational process, the more I saw I did have a choice, it just wasn't the choice I wanted or thought I needed.

I came to see that, by making this choice for change, my partner was loving me. He was loving me so much he was willing to let go and set me free, to make room for our relationship to grow into something new after this particular season had turned. This was a love that had no walls to confine it and it was calling in a place of honoring the evolution of the relationship.

I came to see that the choice I did have was what to make of the transition, that I could choose how to handle it and who I would be at the end of it. A forest burns to create space for new growth. So I began looking at what I was a yes to.

I was a yes to placing to rest the old ways that may have

unconsciously led us to become codependent. I was a yes to acknowledging the ways we were keeping each other smaller than we truly were. Now when you start to own these parts of yourself and the parts of the relationship that demand transitioning, things will start to relax, loosen, and more space is created for something different. Doors will start to open in your life where your purpose, your gifts, your turn-ons are met.

Some may say it is all in the perspective and I would agree. Seeing that I had choices and seeing what they were helped me accept the change in our relationship. However, don't get to thinking that having a new perspective means you get to skip past all the feelings that come with a transition. I do believe wholeheartedly that the human experience is meant to be felt, that it is through feeling that we gather wisdom and information to empower us and assist us in making clear choices. This means mourning and feeling grief, anger, sadness or whatever it may be. The key is feeling it and owning it and not projecting it upon another person.

### *The Ocean of Emotion*

On the evening after our counseling session, my beloved and I sat before each other in this profound place of love, sharing with each other what we appreciated and valued in the other. Our energies created a quiet, soothing environment for us to share our concerns, fears and appreciations. Once the connection was created we were free to speak our truths. Both of us were nervous.

And we recognized that what each of us needed out of our relationship was not aligning. My truth was calling me deeper into devotion or a committed relationship. His truth was calling him to greater sovereignty and independence. Hearing that out loud felt scary. How easy it would have been to override this fear and stay in our current pattern, and in a few months, feel the resentment or anger for not giving ourselves what we needed as sovereign beings…

We cried away the rest of the evening soothing ourselves with bowls full of coconut bliss ice cream and a funny movie, pausing to mourn or cry in each other's arms, questioning the whole while. Yet underneath the pain there was a trusting this was bringing us into right relationship.

To hear from my beloved that we would not be deepening our primary commitment to each other, you can imagine, brought heart wrenching pain, endless tears, confusion, anger, rage and sadness that moved and continues to move in me as I write this.

I can tell you from my own experience that it is like a fucking roller coaster of emotion and confusion, and that after nearly a week of grieving, feeling helpless and confused, and alone along with bouts of anger and rage, I have compassion for why so many people end their relationships unconsciously, choosing to pull away to never talk again. This increased my passion to show you that going into the fire, in the long run, is a more fulfilling way.

Transitioning consciously made me embody what happens emotionally, physiologically, physically, and energetically. It was a storm that seems to be ripping apart everything that we had constructed carefully over the past three and a half years, indeed, everything that I had constructed for the past 45 years since the day I was born.

In February, just before my birthday ritual, my beloved and I flew to Vancouver BC—The land that houses my spirit—to be with my tribe from the north. It was just two short days after we had shared our truths and knew our relationship was changing. Ironically, we just happened to mess up our flight reservations, putting us on different flights from San Diego to Vancouver.

On our day of travel, I woke up on the rage train. The feeling of hate will flow when you embrace and acknowledge it just like any other feeling. I wanted to hate him, I wanted to hate what he was choosing and I wanted to run far away, be in a cave, become a monk and not be near another human being. And I certainly did not want to go to Canada.

Feeling so much anger and rage—to the point where I was feeling hate—was nerve wracking for me. Which is why having a safe environment inside and out to feel this is essential because you can imagine the havoc it has the potential of causing when vomited onto another if one is not clear, present and centered inside of themselves. It is important to not deny these feelings and emotions. There is value in owning them fully.

Emotions are not bad! We have explored throughout this book how emotions have the potential to be one of our greatest allies. It is outdated to think that emotions are bad, better off not seen or heard and inappropriate. However, we have a tendency to slip into old habits when the stress is turned up, and we might get back to believing that emotions are best suppressed right when we need to engage and feel them the most.

I felt the anger and it hurt. I felt scared and it hurt. There was immense discomfort. However in mindful relationships, there is ownership and self responsibility. Upon initially feeling the anger, I walked away and took my space. I know myself and it is important that I have a moment to feel as much as I am able to, and observe my surroundings while I feel without interruption.

For me, being mindful and taking ownership came down to

my strong connection to spirit and my higher self. I sat and had my hate conversations with the spirits as I looked out into the frozen winter rain forests of BC. I hated this decision, I hated the choices my partner was making, I hated the pain, sadness, grief, anger and uncomfortable things I was feeling. I hated the thought that we would not touch each other as we once did. I hated the thought that our rich shamanic transcendent love making would end. I hated it all! I hated the guardedness I was feeling, the sinking in my chest. And during these moments of reflection, introspection and conversations with life, I knew somewhere deep inside that this too would pass, that I was being called in another direction, that there was another area I was being asked to explore for my highest good. And yes, I hated that too!

It was okay to hate all of this, I offered compassion to the hate and to everything that was happening. Hate I believe may be part of the rites of passage of a transition. What is your relationship to hate, do you have a story that you are not supposed to feel it, that it is not sacred? Feel the hate and allow it to flow in a such a way that you own this feeling instead of projecting the hate onto another in violent expression. Try being compassionate to the hate.

## Conscious Transitioning

Conscious transitioning is calling for something new and different. It calls you to trust in and rely upon your personal source. It calls you to love all of yourself and let all of yourself be loved during a period of intense confusion. It calls you to deconstruct all the old victim stories—he/she broke up with me, how could you leave me, how could you do this, why is this happening to me—and see the transition as an opportunity for something new.

You want to acknowledge those victim stories. It may be

as simple as saying "I see you, I feel you and I love you. Thank you for all the ways you served me but I no longer need you. I release." I appreciate getting quiet and saying these words to myself, allowing the feelings to rise and holding myself and all those parts of myself that may be scared. You want to acknowledge that they are in fact stories that were taught to you and reinforced through your previous experiences or what you saw in others. However, you also want to show them through feeling and presence they are loved.

Part of this process is taking ownership for your truth and for your emotions as the empowered person you are. Taking ownership of your truth and emotions can help both of you feel safe in this chaotic sea of feeling. And feeling safe is important. If someone doesn't feel safe in this critical stage, then communication devolves into arguing and blaming, projecting, attacking, or grasping onto to another so you don't drown.

Conscious transition is a dance: separating and coming together, going into stillness and coming back into motion, swaying into and out of these places with awareness.

For me, conscious transitioning was embodied in an image. I had placed my relationship high on an altar to be honored with deep reverence. That relationship was now asking to be taken off the altar. And so I reached up and lifted it, and pulled it towards me. I cradled it before placing it upon the earth as an offering to the spirit, to be recycled into something new, which is in the highest for all beings.

My beloved and I shared five love filled days in Vancouver together. We shared the journey still in partnership, making love, sharing deep care, laughing, crying and also doing a lot of processing. We offered each other presence when things came up and generally enjoyed being together on the journey.

We even said while meandering down 4th street in the rain, that it was so surreal because it felt like it was all a dream and things were the same between us. We laughed, talked, played, loved. Wow! This is possible in such a transition. And it can be confusing.

I looked at my beloved and said "I feel like I want to hate you. I am angry, and I hate what is happening." I felt this little girl's rage inside of me, like I just wanted to pound, kick and scream and fight and force things to be different.

He looked upon me with presence and care and let me know how he understood and how much he loved me. My feelings were real and there was nothing wrong with them nor is there anything wrong with yours. The key is creating a space where you take ownership of them and realize what specifically you are sad, angry and confused about.

## Stillness and Contemplation

Stillness is a friend during such transitions. You may think otherwise, as it seems the normal things to do is get lost in distraction. There is a place for stillness, and a reason for it. Sinking into stillness doesn't meant you get lost in the dark oceans of emotional chaos, it means you watch those emotions, witness them and let them know you are presently in love with them.

Physically, getting into stillness means taking yourself on a vacation, finding someone else to stay with that has a nurturing, healing environment. It means writing, sitting and just observing, meditating, moving your body through dance, walking.

It also means getting clear that nothing needs to be fixed.

I had the ideal situation for me. I was in Canada, completely free to be with my own self. In the home where I was staying, I was surrounded with conscious, mindful people who didn't see me or the situation as being broken. Our trip had been planned since before we started our relationship transition, and it just so happened that I would be staying in Canada for two weeks after my beloved went back home.

Typically my trips to Vancouver are productive, leading workshops, teaching classes, seeing clients. I had planned on finishing up the first draft of my book. But this trip was calling for something different, even though it took me a while to realize that.

When it became clear that we were transitioning, I had a lot of resistance, and I knew it was the little girl inside of me thinking that she needed to stay in control and had to be home and by her man's side to do so. That need to be in control showed up as frustration. I was thinking that I was supposed to be finishing my book, working with clients and making money to support this trip, in essence, following the original plan. But in following that plan, I was essentially arguing with what reality was asking of me.

I was having a chat with a dear soul sister when She noticed I was frustrated. My friend said to me "It's okay to allow this time in Vancouver to be for your personal healing!"

WOW! What a potent reminder and an invitation for me to just let it all be. I realized how much I desired this time to be in reflection on the beauty of the relationship we had shared, to feeling my feelings and return to opening up into my yes for life.

I knew in my core that returning to the relationship I have with myself and nurturing it every day was essential. I knew in the midst of edgy emotions that the key to not allowing them to control you is to be in the present moment. Every time I allowed myself to be still and to feel the full brunt of the story, it all felt safe and I knew I had everything I needed.

*Claiming Space*

Here are some ideas for claiming your space and making the best use of it.

• Create and choose an environment that feels good. Choose one that is healing for you, where you will get appropriate sleep, feel rested, and have no agenda. Choose people around you who don't want to fix you or get caught up in your story. Choose a place that feels womb-like where you have the spaciousness to feel the uncomfortable, the hurts and all the emotional waves and thoughts and still remember who you are as a whole. This is a dance, and when learning this dance you may trip a bit. That is okay. Tripping over your own feet and sometimes your partner's feet is natural when learning a new dance.

   • Have a clear "elevator speech" that you can use to tell others what you are going through. Make it clear that you are not seeking advice, or to have them fix you or the situation, or for them to feel bad for you.

   • Make a list of what fuels you. For me it is having no scheduled agenda, not having to talk, being silent as much as I want, sitting outside, listening to nature, taking long walks in fresh air, and marketing my seminars.

   • Be clear on how long you will need to be in this space. This can change, but having a time frame helps you and those who you are in relationship with.

   • Share with you partner how much you do or don't want to talk to them. For me, I clearly love daily text messages, and daily phone calls just to say hello and share about our days.

- Take it one day at a time.

While you and your partner are taking space, you may have concerns about how to keep the connection open and rich. I want you to know this is natural, especially when your relationship itself is filled with so much love and care. Recognize that a new season is forming and that nothing is wrong, nothing needs fixing.

My invitation to you is to be patient with yourself. This is an incubation time where you are letting the new pattern of your relationship form. During this time you will be asked to step deep into that place of trust inside yourself. It is a time to drop into your own source point, where your fuel comes from within.

## Reuniting

The difference between a relationship transition and a breakup is that in a transition you are making room for the relationship to change and, more importantly, to grow into something new. This is powerful because the new relationship will contain all the intimacy and knowledge of each other that you have shared up until now.

After you have taken some space and got in touch with your own self source again, it is time to reunite, to step back into the things you love, to discover life and learn more about all parts of yourself. I suggest taking these steps to prepare yourselves for this sacred new space you are returning to:

1. Have a clear written list of your needs and requests during this transitional period. Do you need a certain about of space or need to set a maximum as you

transition into conscious companions? What do you want to know about their life? Do you need to step back from knowing or sharing as much as you did when you were in partnership with them? If you are in an open relationship do you want to know about who they are dating or would you prefer knowing nothing?

2. Have code words. I've noticed that challenging communication has moments that process can take a strong hold and every conversation turns into tears. It's upsetting and tiring. When this happens you won't have the energy to be present in your center or to stay in love. Use the code words to gracefully stop a conversation or process if:

   a. It keeps going in circles and the emotions are so heavy the conversation is getting nowhere.

   b. When you know you don't have the capacity to process or go into a certain conversation. It is important that everybody using the code word understands why and what it is. Explain that you want to be present and in love during these tough conversations which is why you use the code word.

3. Make a commitment to show up only for those conversations for which you have the capacity to be present and centered. Tiredness and lack of sleep feed the trigger reaction and will be fuel for argument.

4. Create play time! Yes even in the midst of a relationship transitions play is important to remember. Set time to talk on the phone when it is just about connecting (no processing), go for walks, cuddle, find time to laugh and create your own play time for yourself. This is all essential fuel during these challenging times.

5. Make a schedule. Set times during the week for process or mediated counseling sessions. Have a start-time and end-time. Set boundaries around what is the earliest and latest time of day you will process. Also schedule time for connection.

Sort through together what is appropriate for each of you. One partner may require more or less of any of the things in this list. Find how much you are able to lean in. And find ways and people to whom you can reach out. It will be important that the people you are outsourcing with are able to stay in a clear space, to not give you their opinions or tell you what you should do.

To allow the relationship to grow into its next phase, you will conduct two rituals: one that closes off the last season, honoring the relationship you have shared—and one that opens the next season, the reuniting ceremony.

### Honoring the Relationship You Have Shared

I get excited about ceremony and love the thought of honoring the relationship you have shared up until this point. This may be a new concept to you. In the old paradigm of harsh break ups, blaming each other and getting lost in the he-said-she-said syndrome, you go your separate ways and years down the road you forget what amazing moments you shared in this relationship together.

When two people open their legs, heart, soul and sex to each other, this is a vulnerable place and a gift to share in. You once came together as you opened your union. Your sexual union was a way for your heart and spirit to create inspirational magic for the rest of your life.

Think about when you first met your beloved partner,

what attracted you, what were the moments you shared? Relationships are made up of many ingredients and each one adds flavor to this magnificent meal. What were those ingredients?

Those moments of passionate touch, transcendent sex, deep penetrating eye gazes... When you would get so excited to see your partner walk into a room, no matter who was there and what was happening... These are the moments you want to honor.

You are letting go of the old paradigm that creates separation, suppressions and a repeated pattern of unhealthy relationships (that have been handed down through family and social conditioning). You are creating an empowered way that keeps the love and intimacy you shared in high esteem. It creates space for your primary commitment to soften into being lovers with less time and commitment, or being close friends, or whatever you will grow into.

Before you and your partner come together to honor the relationship you have shared up to now, you will need to find some solo time to do a little bit of homework.

Sit in a comfortable place where you will not be interrupted for a least an hour. Create a sacred space so you feel nourished and held. Make sure to have plenty of tissues, a warm blanket, and pen and paper. For me, I have water or tea and plenty of candles throughout the room.

Close your eyes and start to reflect on your top 10 or 20 experiential highlights within your relationship. Write them down and write down how you felt during the experience.

Take a moment between each one to close your eyes and really imagine you are experiencing it, what needs were met for you during that experience, what feelings were triggered? Breathe deeply. When the tears come, acknowledge them, and acknowledge all the joy and precious moments of love this relationship shared together for the time it was alive.

Write down the way you felt during certain intervals of the relationship. What feelings were awakened in you when you first saw your beloved before you knew them? That first hug or kiss.

Journal about the person you were when you first met and who you are today. How has this relationship empowered you? How have you grown? In what ways are your truths different today than at different points in the relationship?

What were your growth edges? Where did the relationship challenge you but assist you in growth that will impact you both for a lifetime?

Once you have given yourselves as individuals time to go through this journey, set up a time to meet and share what you have written, what you have received through this journey together.

Here you will offer each other and the relationship what I call an extensive appreciation shower. You have shared so much and this is the key to setting each other free to continue to evolve and grow.

Today as I write this, it has been a year and a half since the beginning of my own transition. There is a continuous ebb and flow. It is not a certain, straightforward path. Individuals are different in the time they need during transition, how close they can be through it, and what coming together in a new way will look like. I realized seeing my beloved daily kept me in an emotional loop of neediness with him because of how much affection, care and attraction we shared. So we spent sometimes months interacting only via text, we shared less touch and less flirting but still loads of love. Looking at it today, I can see what served me most was following my dreams and my nomadic heart. I put my life in two suitcases and have made the world my home. Doing what I love most, focusing my attention elsewhere and having some distance actually assisted us in our next phase. We text daily, talk once a week and share immense love.

Honoring all that you have shared up to now marks the closing of the last season of your relationship. Closing this cycle with intention, love and presence helps you show up in a clearer space when you are ready to open the new season. Now your relationship has room to fully enter into the next season. You open that season by performing a reuniting ceremony.

## A New Beginning Ceremony

When you are consciously transitioning there are things to take into consideration. My partner and I were best friends and we wanted to stay connected. We lived together, and we had all intentions of cuddling, even sleeping in the same bed once or twice a week when we felt called, upon the relational shift.

We had many in depth communications to unpack what our bottom lines were, what was serving the body, mind and spirit. When you are transitioning, schedule times to have these conversations, and I would suggest setting a time limit on the conversation. It can be easy to get caught in emotional looping as there is a lot going on here but continue to invite each other into clarity.

What are your personal needs and vision of the reuniting ceremony? What do you and your partner want this new season to look like, what aspects of relating do you want it to contain? Talk about this because your vision is most likely not always the same as your partner's.

Every reuniting ceremony will be different too. You will

have to tailor it to the needs of your relationship. For example, our reuniting ceremony included sexual activity. This may not be appropriate for some who are putting the sexual aspect of their relationship behind them.

For me, I needed a womb like space for a three day period where we could wean ourselves off the old relationship and onto the transition. Each day was about leaning in more to each other and allowing a new relationship to be nursed while an old way of relating was going into hibernation. Our transition took place in the spring.

You must find your way. The key is being with the emotions because they will come in like waves over months, even years depending on the depth and length of your relationship. Prepare the space together. You and your partner are coming together honoring the soul of who you are, honoring the love, the richness, the sex and the magic which was co-created through this union.

We created a lovemaking ceremony. It was going to be a weekend of loving, laughing, crying and enjoying the space in our relationship that was so magical over the past three and a half years. I personally splurged and spent $300 on a hotel room which felt like we were in Spain itself. At home we processed so much; once we were out, our playfulness returned. I felt alive again, like we had been before the emotional processing. It was so healing for our weekend.

Be prepared to bring into the ceremony whatever serves you. We lit candles and shared acknowledgment of what we appreciated about each other, what the relationship inspired in us. We spoke about how we grew together and in ourselves. I created a special video that culminated our journey together, with one of our favorite lovemaking sex songs playing in the background.

We cried and laughed. And the lovemaking began. You want to be prepared if you are choosing to make love and engage sexually as it may be the last time that you are sexual with one another. It is important to be ready for the pain, physical discomfort and emotions that awaken through this dive into each other.

The way that you create this ceremony again will be based on your personal needs, the healthy boundaries you have both set, and the state of mourning your are currently in. Because this process is so individual, I can't set a prescription that works for everyone. However the ideas that follow can give you an idea of what to include or what to avoid for your unique situation.

Set the space for your purpose. Use candles, incense or perfume, and the music of your choice. You may want snacks or something to drink close at hand.

Make sure you have a place where you will not be interrupted. This means considering the noise outside the room. If you live with others you may require getting a room or a vacation home for the weekend. This will be a delicate, tender space, you do not want to rush this experience!

Meditate and get still together. This may mean sitting next to each other or in front of each other for five minutes. Close your eyes and allow yourself to focus on your breath, listening to the sounds and feeling the sensations of what is happening inside your body. Draw your attention to your heart and to a point about two inches below your navel. Visualize your breath moving to the point below your navel and up to your heart and back again. Experience this with ease, not force, for about five minutes. The most important outcome is that you are quieting your mind and getting into feeling present in your body.

Yab Yum. Connect while the man/masculine—or the partner taking this role—sits cross legged, or if hips are tight, with his legs out in a V with a couple of pillows between the legs on the floor close to the pubis. The woman/feminine—or the partner taking that role—slowly approaches her partner, gazing into his eyes and sits on his lap if cross legged or on the cushions if his legs are outstretched. The bottom wraps his arms around the top placing firm support at her lower back and sacrum area. The top places her hands on the back of her partner's heart. Now sitting almost nose to nose, close your eyes and breathe together, allow your bodies to soften and relax more into each other for up to ten minutes. Find that connection with your lower belly up to your heart.

Have your favorite lovemaking music playing. And allow the above breathing together to carry you into an organic natural connection. You may desire at this point to offer your beautiful partner a massage. This evening is to pamper each other and truly awaken how much you really honor and appreciated this journey together. This may be the last time you connect in this way for a while.

Take a couple of gentle deep breaths, start to identify the physical sensations you're having, such as "my chest is tightening," or "my body feels contracted." Do your best to identify what you are feeling. "I am feeling scared, sad, angry and confused." The person, your partner who is on the other side of this conversation may simply take a moment to acknowledge these feelings which you are having without trying to strategize or fix anything.

Be prepared and understand that this experience may not be filled with lightness, joy or even pleasure. It may be overlaid with outpourings of grief, sadness, and anger. You may experience physical discomfort upon penetration if you choose to have sex. Remember back in earlier chapters as we covered the topics of emotional armoring and how the body holds onto the emotional pains, and traumas.

I recall the moment my partner penetrated me, my inner walls of my vagina felt raw as I was having some excessive internal heat in my body. It was a reaction to all the emotional stress during this time of change. There were waves of rich pleasure and there were heart opening moments where the only thing that would come through were tears and sorrow along with the expansive love. When our hearts are open we feel more. When I orgasmed it was a combination of sobbing, and boisterous cries of multidimensional pleasure. We held each other so tightly after, breathing together and being mindful of the tenderness of this moment and of each other's heart.

Suddenly I was paying attention to my internal process, feeling my chest begin to contract, my guard begin to go up, and all these questions flooding out. What do I do now, how do I do it? Why are you choosing this, when did things break, how can it be so easy for you? The self torture session continued. Then came the awareness that his parents would ask about me and us and that they would soon know. This was the moment that I began to accept things were really changing.

This is a wonderful moment to pause, use those communication tools to let your partner know what's happening in a simple sentence and that you need to just pause. You want to share what you are feeling emotionally and how the body and mind are reacting. Pay attention if the story is so covered in panic that you get lost in the spin of endless blaming. This is the self responsibility part.

For me, even though part of me wanted to hate him, I still deeply loved him. I was angry that he did not choose deepening in the style of relationship I was ready for. I was angry that things were changing. I was angry that he was not willing to love me the way I was ready to be loved, even though he loved me. I was confused and unclear about what was going to happen.

Remember there is nothing broken and that this will take time and care. Especially taking into consideration how long that last rich, deep season may have lasted.

When you are clear on what you are feeling it assists your partner in feeling safe and also connected with you. If you are in a ball of chaos, it creates contraction in your body and reactions towards the other which would ultimately create disconnection. What we are encouraging here is connection, to feel safe and to remember you are loved. However your ceremony plays out, communication is key.

We began Revolutionizing Intimacy with the breath. As life starts when the breath starts and ends when the breath ends, so this book comes full circle. As the ceremony comes to a close, and you bid farewell to the last season of your relationship, you must return to nurturing the relationship you have with yourself—you return to the beginning of this book and return to the nurturing and life-long relationship you have with your breath. Your breath is the intelligence which holds powerful information for you to shift your conditioned past, to return back to your personal power and sensual vitality.

# Going the Distance

For me, navigating a relationship is one of the highest forms of spiritual practice. When we allow the relationship to be our teacher we have the ability to create such profound change and expansive growth in our own selves. When we move beyond what we call new relationship energy (the chemical high associated with increased neurotransmitter activity for the first year or so), we move into the deep stages of sacred partnership.

I was having a conversation with a friend the other day about relationships. He was sharing about how relationships are so challenging and such work. I understood his perspective. I began to explain how for many of us, after the excitement of a new relationship starts to fade, the really juicy shadowy pieces come up. All the conditionings from upbringing and family starts to surface. I can clearly see when the little girl in me wants things a certain way. I know, from cultivating that deep relationship with myself, when old emotions and traumas are triggered. Sometimes we get so taken by them it can be challenging to know what is real right now versus what is bubbling up in us from our past. This can be painful, especially when the people relating do not understand this, they don't have the skills or awareness to move beyond this or realize there is another way.

If our eyes and hearts are open enough, we share our path with another or others in such a way that we meet in the middle. It becomes about how our own unique self can meet another in their own unique self. Together each day we evolve in our understanding of each other and of ourselves. When the relationship is healthy with self-responsible, emotionally mature people, our shadow side has a place to rise up, and be witnessed, and in so doing, it can become the grounds for such deep transformation and insight. Those places that most run from in a relationship, the ebbs and flows, ups and downs, become our teachers.

How open do we choose to be in our personal evolution? Are we able to acknowledge our shadows? Can we see the little girl or boy that comes out in our adult relationship because of old conditioning? Are we able to look at ourselves just as we are being triggered and ask "what is this showing me about myself?" Might we transform judgment of another into curiosity? When we are upset or in disagreement in our relationships it does not mean the relationship is over. I see it as an opportunity to say, share more please, I desire to learn and understand you so I may understand myself more.

In this stage of relating, we get to tune into our own passion, creativity and joy—as it is no one else's job to give this to us. From this place, we get to create fun dates, ways of sharing what is exciting for us. We can talk about what turns us on and create date nights that include sexual exploration and things we love.

When you're in it to go the distance, relationships stop being about that white picket fence, and they lose that awful notion that "you complete me." You are already complete! A healthy long relationship lets the participants walk together, empowered in who each of them is. It raises the questions "how may I evolve to live clearer, more centered and aware," and "how can we allow this love of relating to bring about greater good in the world?"

Remember that the quality of relationship you enjoy with others stems from the quality of the relationship you have with yourself. Sometimes in the best of relationships you get so caught up in the buzz of the relationship you find yourself one day not knowing what energizes you, what you are passionate about doing, what things you did for fun before getting into this relationship.

## *Relationship Beyond the New Relationship High*

New relationship energy (NRE) is a high we all have felt more than once to be certain. You know that moment you look across the room, your eyes meet, your heart starts racing and this euphoric state rushes through the body. Over the next months and into the first year or two, this new relationship grabs all your attention, and offers up passion, excitement and borderline infatuation.

Falling in love can be one of the most addictive experiences on earth. Once you have had a taste of NRE, a craving for more sets in. During NRE the chemicals in the brain get switch into high drive. Falling in love has been compared to being on cocaine. Serotonin, norepinephrine and dopamine all play important roles during NRE, with a reduction in serotonin and an increase in the latter two. (It is also known that those who experience obsessive compulsive disorders also have low levels of serotonin which has scientists speculating at the similarities in one's actions during NRE and being obsessive compulsive.)

The brain chemistry that accompanies NRE will last between 18 months and 3 years. As we ucage intimacy we build awareness of how we may honor the natural rhythms of relationships. Part of that awareness means understanding that what is taking place inside of us has a neurochemical basis[10].

---

[10] Science in the News Blog; "Love, Actually: The science behind lust, attraction, and companionship," blog entry by Katherine Wu, figures by Tito Adhikary, February 14, 2017, http://sitn.hms.harvard.edu/flash/2017/
love-actually-science-behind-lust-attraction-companionship/

Sometimes this can offer a peace of mind when we are feeling buffeted by the strong emotions of new love.

As relationships evolve into what I call "mature love" the passion and joy to share together expands into more depth of bonding, enjoyment of the quiet moments, and has a gentler, rooted connection. Some have called this the "attachment phase" where the two hormones most closely associated appear to be oxytocin and vasopressin.

Mature love deepens the bond you share as the connection you have ages gracefully like a fine wine. It is quite different from NRE and beautiful in its own right. Experiencing mature love is warm and comforting, like a womb of comfort.

### *How to Relate with Someone Who Is Not Honoring Their Truth*

Imagine you have a friend who is a constant pushover. You see them continually giving more than they really want to as a way to please others or get more attention. This leaves them drained and frustrated and complaining about it to you. Or perhaps you're in a relationship and your partner makes choices every day that do not honor or value the health and wellbeing of their body. They continually talk about getting out for a jog, joining a gym and going out to apply for that new job that really excites them, however they never take action. They end up as a less than present partner. Failing to honoring their deep truth—what their heart truly calls out to them—weighs on the communication, the sex and the intimacy you share.

That same behavior is a lot edgier when your partner is not honoring their truth when it comes to the relationship. What do you do when you clearly see the relationship is not serving your partner's soul-call or where their journey is taking them?

Our hearts ache whenever we come to see that our partner's truths is calling them in a different direction from our own. Love sets a person free; it is not a cage to keep them like some prize trophy, responsible for your happiness. It is a very vulnerable moment when you have so much invested, and you see your partner's truth before they are ready to admit it to themselves.

Honoring our individual truth is actually a gift to the relationship. It allows the relationship to change and grow organically into something that best serves each person so their heart and spirit may fully soar. Life is so short. The old codependency of relationships makes love into a cage and keeps it locked no matter what.

When someone you love is not honoring their truth it is a great time to amp up your own self responsibility. Get super clear, access the compassion and turn up the emotional intelligence volume. Set up a time to have communication that you know will touch areas of vulnerability. Use your communication skills and get curious about the other person's truth, what ignites their heart and spirit. The more these conversations happen the more often awareness on their part builds of their truth and brings to light where they have not shown up for it.

You may be absolutely clear and ask them why they have stopped doing what their heart and spirit really want? You may state "I have noticed you don't seem as passionate about various things that used to be important to you, is this true?"

Set a time limit and clear agreement for yourself. What is your bottom line? If your friend or partner continues to not own, and takes no steps towards being proactive in living their truth, how will it affect your relational choices, how long are you willing to accept that impact?

Setting a bottom line means you have decided in advance

how much of your partner's behavior you are willing to tolerate before they come into alignment with what's right for them. It is a way to honor your own truth about what you need in a good healthy relationship. If the situation gets to that final straw, you will make a decision to follow your inner truth and honor the relationship and your partner by consciously transitioning.

## Repairing Broken Trust — A New Perspective

Trust gets broken in all kinds of ways in a relationship. A person strays outside of a clear monogamous agreement, having sex with another without permission. Someone forces a sexual situation past the other's boundary and into nonconsensual sex. You share something confidentially with a friend and the next thing you know the entire community has heard it. These broken agreements trigger wounded feelings that limit and block intimacy in any relationship.

Broken trust may be the toughest situation you can face in a relationship because it pushes really big buttons; it feels like someone just doesn't care. We all carry known and unknown wounded stories locked away in our memories. So we often enter into relationships with feelings of deceit, abandonment, rejection or other humiliations from the past hidden just below the surface, waiting to be triggered again. It is understandable that a broken trust situation feels as if someone just ripped the scab of a wound and poured salt onto it.

Those old wounds hurt, and we often find ourselves yearning for that one person to fill the void that the wound dug in so deep. Humans are all too easily persuaded to put all their faith upon the altar of another human. You may have noticed attracting a person who at first soothed the pains. Yet when they began doing things that did not meet the need of that past hurt, you began to feel consumed and unsafe again. Even with the best intentions, counting on another to soothe those pains can actually be the most disempowering act, and a tiring one for the person who accepts the role as the all-mighty one. It sets expectations that can easily lead to broken trust.

Broken trust feels like an intractable problem. If someone doesn't care or isn't trustworthy, how can you trust them in whatever solution you come up with to the trust that was broken in the first place? They have shown you, after all, that they are capable, even likely to break someone's trust.

Suppressing and not dealing with the wounded feelings that arise will only keep someone in misery for the rest of their life, creating unconscious beliefs and limiting stories that they will carry forever. Rather than suppressing I am inviting you to own them and be proactive in your choices. This is very hard because it calls for you to be really, radically self-responsible. It call for you to see the situation from a very different perspective, one that is subtle and hard to grasp.

To get you thinking about this perspective, I want you to think on the saying "If you don't trust yourself, you likely will not be able to trust another."

Your first reaction is probably "well, of course I trust myself! But others have betrayed me in the past." But there is subtlety in this. For example, do you trust yourself to never make an agreement that is impossible to break? No? Then how could you trust another to never break an agreement you have made?

We will come back to this new perspective, but first let me share a story with you about my own response to broken trust and radical self responsibility.

I have been in open relationships and there were often times where myself and my lover's lovers or potential lovers did not have a great connection. Whether it was different a value system or having nothing in common, for some emotional reason there were triggers. There was one woman in particular that I remember that I had a challenging time with.

I acknowledged the resistance I had around her interacting with my lover and I wanted to lean in and get curious to learn more about her. We went to dinner one night where my personal intention was to be as vulnerable with her as possible, to share with her my fears and my concerns and I even had some requests. She was attracted to a lover of mine and I desired to get to know her more before they acted on it. We talked and I expressed my fears. I asked her to keep from advancing the situation with my lover until we had gotten to know each other better and until we developed a deeper friendship. That felt really good, it felt safe. Quality time is a way I perceive that people care.

After dinner we went out with a group of friends. In the midst of a very large, public social event the group started getting into some intimate conversations. The next thing I knew this woman was very loudly stating how much she wanted to have sex with that lover of mine. I will tell you my natural reaction was wanting to protect as I felt so unsafe in that moment. Even though I did my best to keep smiling, my face turned red, and panic started to set in. Silently my head whirled with thoughts. How could she, why would she, does she lack that much awareness? We had just had a vulnerable conversation about my fears and she just stuck a knife in an open wound.

This is a small example of what some may call "broken trust," but it is none the less broken trust, or better yet "where someone else did not live up to my expectations." I had shared with her an expectation that she would do things in a way where I felt safe and had my needs considered. What got triggered in me were my old emotional stories of abandonment and betrayal which had nothing to do with this woman. In reflection, I actually believe she was just being her playful, free loving self and lacked the awareness to keep in mind what I had expected and requested. We related differently but it was not that she intentionally did anything to me or to break anything.

After this situation I dove into my own radical self responsibility. I owned my emotional tenderness, created boundaries which meant taking space from this person, not out of anger but out of giving myself what I needed. There is a big difference. I unpacked and investigated what feelings were there and where the core of it came from. I also did the inner work to process on an energetic and emotional level. A part of me was coming up to be transformed and she was only the messenger. It was such an opportunity for me.

Something to remember is that I am not offering a way to determine what is or who was right or wrong in your personal situation. To focus on that is to miss the incredible opportunity here, and to miss the new perspective. What I am offering is a way to greater freedom and self liberation, a way to wellbeing and health. If you stay angry who are you hurting? There is a good chance the other has moved on having forgotten the situation or never was aware of the hurt in the first place, and you are contracted, tense and angry. What I am offering is a way to get clear, understand your feelings and needs, so that you are able to be proactive and set clear boundaries making choices now that serve your wellbeing and your future relationships. This might mean walking away from the situation, the friendship, the relationship, the business partnership.

When we say things like "How could you do that to me, I trusted you?" What we are really saying is "I feel hurt, sad and angry because you did not live up to my expectations and fulfill my needs and desires."

Getting at the root of the feeling of broken trust requires a shift in perspective, going from "you broke our trust" to "I feel disappointed, sad and angry because I was needing or wanting _____." This will set the healing process in a clearer direction for you to take back your power. This is about you and your moving forward beyond broken trust. After all, the quality and integrity of your relationships flows from, indeed mirrors, the relationship you have with yourself. And you cannot change the relationship someone else has with their own self. So let's turn our attention to what you can work with.

Often when we feel our trust was broken, we get stuck in a story, blaming, pointing the finger. "Someone did this to me. how dare they?!" Broken trust is such a deep violation that it sends our emotions into high gear and puts us in the fight, flight or freeze response. While it can be easy to get lost in the pain of the wound while going deeper into the abyss of the raging emotions when the limbic system is on high drive, I highly suggest remembering your best practices to do the opposite. To get past the broken trust, you will want to pause, to self source by taking reflective space and come into the truth of what has triggered the experience of broken trust. This path takes courage.

To help you disengage the fight response, bring attention to your breath, pause and observe your feelings. These two actions will help calm the nervous system and keep you from getting lost in explosive impulsive reactions.

**The first step in transforming the pain of a broken agreement is solo work.** You will want to go into the uncomfortable feelings and get clear on the nature of those feelings. It can be easy to get lost in blaming or attacking another, or freezing and loosing your voice and suppressing what's there. If the wound goes unaddressed, it will fester and build resentment in you. If you want to move through this situation so it does not weigh you or your future experiences down again, you must unpack your feelings. Write in your diary or journey from a radically honest perspective. Once you have purged the story, allow it to help you get clear on your feelings, and what you were and are needing.

To get yourself started, ask yourself these questions and write down the answers:

- What am I presently feeling?
- Does this situation trigger previous memories, past pains or beliefs about myself or others?
- What am I needing right now?
- What was I needing when I felt the trust was broken?

You may want to consider individual coaching or counseling in this process to help you work past your old conditioning or wounds.

Remember to self-sooth. Place yourself in environments that affirm you are loved, valuable, cared for and cherished. And treat yourself somehow—get a massage, go for a float, dress up and do what uplifts your spirits.

After the solo process is finished, it is time to get all the people involved coming together in a compassionate communication process. All parties are choosing to be self-responsible and radically honest throughout this process. Depending on the subject at hand, you may break the process into steps with pauses in between rather than getting it all done at once. The aim here is to look past the stories we make about the broken trust.

**The second step is sharing the feelings and needs of all people.** You may believe or feel the person at hand did what they did just to be cruel and hurt you, but they too have needs which is what lead them to break an agreement. We are not here to say one side is right and the other is wrong. We are here to get honest, blow up expectation, own our feelings and create resolution. Don't let agreements become a prison sentence.

This is not an easy process because we are so apt to slip into old wounded patterns. Do your best to stay curious to yourself and to the other person's experience. Slow the process down and use those Deep Listening skills.

**The third step is acknowledgment.** There wants to be acknowledgment of hurt feelings and unmet needs both by yourself and by the other people involved. We are not taking or assigning blame here, rather we are trying to truly empathize with the person hurting. Your heartfelt feelings show that you really feel and see that what they are feeling is real.

This is an ideal time to practice the art of apology. Acknowledging the pain of another, their unmet need or unfulfilled desire is essential. This is not done from a place of self-shaming or assigning blame, but from a place of deep compassion. The point is to acknowledge those feelings of hurt and betrayal.

This is also an ideal time to practice radical honesty—for the one who broke the agreement, OWN IT! Verbally share exactly what the actions were which broke the agreement.

This may be a good place to take a break. You may find more feelings coming up and I invite you to take your own space for 24 to 48 hours to reflect on the feelings and needs of all before moving forward.

**The fourth step is to rebuild.** In this phase, you create new agreements based on a new and deeper understanding of each other's needs. This is the hardest step. Don't rush this process. Be honest with how much space you may need before moving forward into new agreements. Schedule time to communicate. Setting a time creates a sense of safety and can allow one's nervous system to calm down especially when in a trigger. Mediation can assist in opening to the "dual perspective."

In past relationships you may have had the idea that after someone breaks your trust, promises need to be made to not hurt you again. Not being hurt again is a good hope, a good aim, but it is an awful promise to expect from someone. If you want someone to promise not to hurt you, you are holding the other person or people responsible for your feelings. In that, you disempower yourself. And that promise is vague and expansive; who knows what might hurt you in the future, who could possibly know or predict all your triggers? Rather getting clear on what "not being hurt" means for you gives the other person the space to understand what you're really needing and they can make an empowered choice if they are able to help fulfill that need. A broken agreement clearly shows that the original expectation is not a fit anymore.

"But wait," you might be screaming, "doesn't this mean I have to trust the other person? I can't, they just broke my trust!" Or you might be asking "Doesn't this dilute any agreement to the point where it is meaningless?" It does not mean either of those things. This new perspective, this dive into radical self responsibility is a way to invite this other person in to do the same. If you are so radically honest about what your needs and feelings and experiences are without holding another responsible for those things, you invite them to comport themselves the same way. You set a standard for the kind of interaction you want to have with them. You can use your own ownership of the situation as a demonstration for the kind of behavior and perspective you value and desire in the people you interact with.

In this new perspective, don't hurt me really may mean, please be honest me even if a business or personal agreement is not working out, be honest if you have different needs that are not being met in this current partnership both personally or professionally, please share more affection with me, please verbally share why you appreciate me on a daily or weekly basis to rebuild and nourish our connection. Requesting communication when something isn't working prior to taking action that may elicit feelings of broken trust becomes a priority.

Creating new agreements or a new platform as I like to call it takes into account all people's feelings and needs. This is a process which may be explored if all people involved are a yes to it. Bring your unspoken needs and feelings to the table. Make sure everyone involved in this communication is in a place that they can be present, listen to the other, share feeling honesty. Mediation may be useful here.

Creating a new platform means rather than expecting or demanding someone to not hurt you again, you get clear on what you are needing. Go ahead and unpack this. What are the actions that you feel hurt by? Also unpack what hurt is to you.

If not all the people are in a place to rebuild the collaboration or relationship, the biggest self responsible, proactive thing you could do may be to walk away. Choosing love may mean it is time to set yourself and the other person or people free. It may mean that processing through the broken agreement or unmet expectation is something you have to do without them. This would be a perfect time to do a solo communication process in a journal, getting clear on your own feelings and needs along with relational values. If you have to walk away from a relationship, it means you do it from a clear space with the highest good in mind instead of from a reactive angry space.

The idea of betrayal is inevitable in a world where we set

others up to our expectations and ideals, where we make others responsible for the way we feel or for holding us back from living fully. Remember earlier we spoke about how change happens moment by moment. Relationships and people change. Your needs today will be different a few years down the road as with your friends or partner, personally or professionally. Broken agreements take place when these feelings, needs and changes can no longer be suppressed or denied.

When we realize that change is inevitable and that likely those we share life with will do something that we disagree with or that doesn't match our own needs we can finally exhale. We can choose to respond differently. Let go of the control button! This would be a time to commit to yourself, get curious, build a life where you are committed to get to know all sides of yourself daily, as well as your partner's, friend's and colleague's needs and desires. Getting to know them only means more intimacy and greater personal freedom. Note it does not mean you have to agree with these parts or other's choices but by getting curious to understanding you are undoing the idea of betrayal and choosing more compassion and space for relationships to evolve and grow. You are turning these experiences into processes to grow and learn.

# Polyamory and Alternative Relationship Choices

People are on such unique journeys that the definition of a relationship cannot be constrained to one cookie-cutter formula. The intentions of this book is to fundamentally change how we view and experience intimacy, so I believe it's important to briefly look at some of the relationship models that are a little less traditional. While this book is not the platform to dive into the full scope of this topic, the discussion here should be enough to prompt you to do a little research if you feel called.

These relationship styles exist because they better align with the needs of those involved. Note that all of these relationship styles discussed here follow the principle of being entirely consensual. That means all the people involved are aware of other lovers or partners and other relationships or sexual ties. This is quite different from being in an agreed monogamous relationship and going behind your partner's back to have a secret affair.

If we are going to uncage intimacy we must be aware that we no longer live in a tight closed box of monogamy and heterosexual relating. That is not to say that any one way is better than the others, and it does not mean any of these alternative styles of relating are for you.

Here are some alternative relationship configurations outside of the traditional monogamy platform.

Open relating or polyamory — The philosophy or state of being in love or romantically involved with more than one person at the same time: multiple consensual concurrent relationships. This can include one primary relationship with other secondary ones, or can have all relationships with the same priority.

**Solo-poly** — A person considers their relationship with their own self to be their primary relationship (in place of a primary partner). All other relationships are secondary, though not necessarily equal.

**Swinging** — Swinging (or partner swapping) is a completely non-monogamous behavior in which a couple in a committed relationship swaps partners to engage in sexual activity.

**Triadic** — Being in a consensual bonded relationship with three people of the same or mixed genders. It may look like a monogamish style where all three in the relationships share what deeply bonded couples share.

Navigating Alternative Relationship Choices

In the world of alternative relationships it is common that all of your lovers will not exactly see eye to eye. However in my experience this is an opportunity for growth for all involved. Ignoring the differences is a huge fire hazard which will eventually lead to a deadly explosion. So what do you do if your partner's lovers have different poly styles and views?

First, turn to yourself. As with all of the conflict we have addressed in this book, the resolution germinates from within your own self. Do the work, uncover your stories, clear your past emotional wounding. Self inquiry and daily breath work have been an essential part of my life path in staying clear every day. Not only is this part of my morning ritual, I also do it before I delve into any particularly intense conversations. It opens us up to clarity and allows our communication to be responsible and come from the heart.

Second, find ways to continue to dive deep into your primary relationship. Wake up each day with a gratitude list for the fullness of your cup and everything you are sharing. Share appreciation showers, reassurance and acknowledgments daily.

Have FUN! It is essential that we realize our heart's unique connection with each partner individually.

Third, find a way to ensure everyone involved is able to feel understood. It means moving away from right and wrong and really being curious with a desire to understand. Find where you all can agree on a middle ground. This requires you to really hone and tap-in to your Deep Listening skills to be able to understand what your partners are experiencing and feeling.

This is a two way street, and to help your partners understand your experience, you must communicate your own experience fully and transparently. I find that when you are fully transparent in your communication it eliminates so much misunderstanding.

Regardless of the style of relationship I have been in, transparent conscious communication has always been a life saver for me (and my partners). This may be more or less natural for you than the others in your relationship. Reach out, be emotionally responsible and transparently communicate what you are needing from yourself and the others.

When I can be self-responsible for and transparent about my feelings it enables me to respond with a sincere "Thank you for sharing and telling me about your upcoming play date. I love and appreciate you being so transparent with me. It assists me in feeling included and special. I feel a little nervous in my body though and a little bit scared of this new unknown experience, yet I feel really connected with you right now." This opens me up to such profound intimacy.

Can you see how this conversation and the approach allows a safe space for hearts to open, creating deeper intimacy and realizing the extraordinary love that exists in this relationship?

You have probably figured it out already, but I'll say it anyway. Even though I am speaking of open, non-traditional relationships, these ideas are just as powerful if you apply them to a monogamous partnership, to friendships and even to business relationships.

We can all say it is all about love—and it is. Part of love is self care and acknowledging where we are at in our human evolution. It takes graceful ease and nourishment, not force, to cultivate open relationships.

I will be the first to acknowledge that this way of being and living can be very edgy and can bring up intense feelings. But it also has a way of granting the grandest of miracle of all: relating from a place where fear no longer controls us.

# An Intimate Relationship with Existence Itself

Wow! You have worked your way through a tremendous amount of material to get to this point in the book. And if you have been engaging proactively, then you have also done a tremendous amount of work on yourself and your relationships. I commend you for that. How would you feel if I told you that all the work you've done and the skills you have built—communication, conscious touch, intentional sexuality, tapping into your power—was all superficial and not the true aim of this book? All of these tangible skills and ways of interacting are invaluable and are essential to living in an intimately connected way. I have taught these skills and lessons for nearly two decades, but they are not the end. They are merely the door!

The true essence of this book, the place it aims is that place where we merge with all things, where there is no separation and we allow life itself to penetrate us, permeate us to the core of our being. This is the place I have been speaking about throughout my career. And over the past two decades I have been diving deeper and deeper into this place on my own personal journey.

I remember back into my childhood, feeling like the oddball, many of the children teasing me, calling me names and solidifying for me the idea that I just did not fit in. I was confused because I had no one to talk to about this. I didn't have the skills and didn't feel safe to understand what it meant to lean into my body, my emotional self and my sensitivity to life, let alone leaning into other people for love.

I am grateful, though, that early on in my twenties this changed for me. I began to attract wise mentors and guides who would take me under their wings as an apprentice and help me start to cultivate this new found relationship with myself and life. My heart began to blossom and the curiosity which I felt as a child began to expand immensely.

For two decades now, I have lead circles, presented workshops, conducted multi-day seminars, and held space for individuals and couples all around the world. I have studied the breath, sacred sexuality, divine partnership, tantra, conscious touch, compassionate communication, radical honesty, and empathy development. I have cultivated presence and mindfulness, and turned my relationships with everything—food, exercise, empowerment, other people—into a spiritual practice. I have gone on, and conducted other rich transformational shamanic journeys. This has been my life.

Even in the evolution of my personal and professional life, it still comes back to the question, to what degree are you able to really feel life permeate you? Are you able to allow your entire person to feel as if it dissolves, leaving something that is strong and integral at its core and yet soft in its shell? Are you able to feel like there are no barriers between you and life?

This is an interesting sensation to feel. And as I write, I wonder will anyone understand in their bodies what I am speaking about? Shouldn't attaining this deep intimacy with existence itself be the all important piece in our experience of life?

The thing is, that experience is so far removed from the day-to-day routine that our culture allows us, that it is hard to even articulate that there is such an experience just waiting for us. So, we have to look to the intermediate steps, and that is what this book has been about.

I do it, I use marketing language to reach my audience. I have used phrases like, have better sex, attract the relationships you desire, cultivate communication skills. I focus on the top layer, speaking in a way that is familiar so as to open the door for others to grow and then learn about those deeper and deeper skills.

Now it is true that these top layer skills are some of the tangible outcomes of this work and are immensely valuable, but please don't stop there. This is not the end point; there is so much more! You can have more than just better physical relationships. You can share understanding that is deeper than being seen and heard.

I want you to know you can actually feel as if life, nature and all things are penetrating you. Is it not important to feel this in-touch, in-tune, alive and turned-on to life? Do you get lost in the superficial layers of bliss and stop diving deeper into your evolution?

For me it is all important and invaluable that life permeate me in every moment. During a 13 day silent Vipassana meditation, my whole being felt the awareness that, as human beings, we are merely scratching the surface of the intimate relationships which is possible with existence itself.

Let's remember all the teachings and practices I have spoken about are the doorway to access such deep layers of yourself. Cultivating a relationship with these teachings and experiences are essential. They are your stepping stones to creating a more in-tuned, aware, lighter version of yourself. The skills which you begin to use in your daily relationships are also stepping stones. As you being to act in new ways towards yourself and others it builds a more transparent state of being. Physically you start to engage life with a more relaxed nervous system, a steady clear mind, and fluidity in your body. Your energy flows more easily and this will soon take you beyond using these tools to get the relationship you desire or to have a clearer conversation. It will take you into a strange synthesis where life itself becomes you. That life penetrates you, and you feel that everything lives within you. It becomes corporeal knowledge, not just a concept you have read or get with your mind, not just something you think is a cool new age fad. But when you really open up from a healthy integral place, your choices and the way you live will naturally change. Now whenever you do something, you consider the whole. You meet every moment with a new found light.

This means children and adults begin to embrace each other in ways that are all welcoming. It means no more feeling or speaking harm upon others, no more nit picking or laughing when you don't understand another. It means opening up a deep body-sense of curiosity because you realize that understanding is the way through the door.

This is a what I mean when I speak of Revolutionizing Intimacy!

# About the Author

Tziporah Kingsbury, founder of the Soulful Relating Institute, is a renowned pioneer and innovator in the realm of intimate exploration and personal expression.

As an intimacy, breath work, and communication leader, creator of the Soulful Relating 7-Step system, she innovates specialized and personally-tailored programming.

For nearly two decades Tziporah has dedicated her life and work to devloping the skills and practices found in Revolutionizing Intimacy, choosing to cultivate a profound relationship with body, mind, sexuality, and spirit — and to teaching people just like you to do the same!

Tziporah's passion is guiding people from all walks of life to cultivate their most potent personal self-expression in their relationships and work lives. Author of the pocket-sized Intimate Insights, she has been coined "The Love Guru" On ABC's The Bachelor in 2015.

While she began her professional career as a competitive bodybuilder and health and fitness educator, a health crisis caused an awakening in her that changed her life path forever. She began training in the ways of Mindfulness, Breathwork, Tantra, Human Relating and Communication extensively across the globe, eventually becoming a peer to her instructors.

All the discipline, determination and presence of mind she had utilized as an athlete was devoted towards finding radical authenticity in relationships, cultivating emotional intelligence, holding a vulnerable loving heart in all situations and to prioritizing joy, self-nurturance and the intense pleasure she found in her personal purpose.

Her own journey has allowed Tziporah to specialize in guiding other consciously-minded leaders, entrepreneurs, and couples to awaken their spiritual, sensual and sexual aliveness, so they can create profound relationships "from the bedroom to the boardroom." She continues to be called upon by other new thought leaders as well as organizations and corporations to share her expertise in the areas of emotional intelligence and mindful relating as an inspirational speaker.

Tziporah is versed in many modalities and designed the Soulful Relating 7-Step System as a comprehensive way to truly create and sustain new ways of conscious living and relating in her client's lives.

**Why the world needs Revolutionizing Intimacy NOW!**

Twenty years ago I was so disconnected and stressed that my body literally shut down. I knew it was time to change or die. I chose change. I set off on a journey and realized that we live in a world where we feel compelled to be connected and to constantly make things happen. In our drive for these very ideals, though, we end up creating a vicious cycle.

We create disconnections, first within ourselves and then with others. Our personal relationships, home lives, and even our work environments suffer.

- We experience separation globally and interpersonally.
- We compete instead of uplift.
- We seek relationships to try to fill a void.
- We get caught up in blame, shame, judgment, and finger pointing.

The good news is we can shift the consciousness around the way we relate… and return to the intimate, loving creatures we are meant to be in every aspect of our lives. It's time for change! Living burdened by emotional shame, chasing relationships to fill an empty void, and living overstimulated is tearing us all apart. We find it normal to feel disheartened and depressed. I know from experience, this kind of "life" is no longer an option!

# Additional Resources and Charts

**The Seven Adjustments™**

Resistance — Willingness
Make Wrong — Curiosity
Judgment — Compassion
Guilt — Acceptance
Blame — Understanding
Shame — Reassurance
Criticism — Appreciation

**Moving from Pain & Fear to Love**

## Ask yourself:

1. Am I **willing** to practice new ways of thinking, listening and expressing?
2. Am I genuinely **curious** to know what is 'real' for the other?
3. Can I feel **compassion** for the pain of unmet needs on both sides?
4. Am I **willing** to **acept** what is so just as it is?
5. What authentic **reassurance** can I provide to the others?
6. What might I offer or request that would demonstrate my **understanding** of their feelings, needs and commitments?
7. What can I **appreciate** myself and the other for?

# What is Alive in Me?

The Essence
Of Being
Is Love

The Field
Of Infinite
Possibility

What are you telling yourself that is generating these feelings?

Every challenge life brings is an opportunity to flex your spiritual muscle. What qualities of light are you inspired to practice?

Egoic Thinking:

Blaming
Shaming
Demanding
Criticizing
Accusing
Judging
Evaluating
Analyzing
Labeling
Better than
Worse than
Dominating
Being a Victim
Right/Wrong
Me Vs. You

Universal Needs
and Values:

Joy
Love
Respect
Empathy
Gratitude
Compassion
Forgiveness
Gentleness
Reassurance
Acceptance
Understanding
Trustworthiness
Being Abundant
Cooperation
Win/Win

At the heart
of every behavior
is the desire to meet
a precious need.

Clouds the Light
and Creates
Separation

Bring Forth the Light:
Energy of Life
& Creates Peace

What are your unmet needs and/or egoic thinking:

Unpleasant feelings are signs of unmet need.

It's All Love
Or A Call For Love

Feelings Are
The Way In To The Heart

© 2010 Christy Michaels & Katrina Vaillancourt • info@sunrise-center.org

261

# Emotions Inventory

The following are the words we use when we want to express a combination of emotional states and physical sensations. This reduced list is neither exhaustive nor definitive. It is meant as a starting place to support anyone who wishes to engage in a process of deepening self-discovery and to facilitate greater understanding and connection between people.

## Emotions when your needs/values/longings are not satisfied

**AFRAID**
frightened
scared
suspicious
terrified
worried

**ANNOYED**
frustrated
impatient
irritated

**ANGRY**
hate
shocked
surprised
upset
violent

**CONFUSED**
hesitant
torn

**EMBARRASSED**

**DISCONNECTED**
bored
distant
indifferent
numb
uncomfortable
withdrawn

**TIRED**
exhausted
sleepy

**SAD**
depressed
despair
disappointed
discouraged
grief
heartbroken
hurt
lonely
nostalgic
regretful

**TENSE**
anxious
irritable
nervous
overwhelmed
stressed out

**VULNERABLE**
guarded
insecure
sensitive

## Emotions when your needs/values are satisfied

**AFFECTIONATE**
compassionate
loving
open
warm

**ENGAGED**
curious
interested

**HOPEFUL**
encouraged
optimistic

**CONFIDENT**
empowered
open
proud
safe
secure

**EXCITED**
aroused
eager
enthusiastic
passionate

**GRATEFUL**
moved
touched

**INSPIRED**

**JOYFUL**
delighted
happy
ecstatic
elated

**REFRESHED**
renewed
rested

**PEACEFUL**
calm
clear headed
comfortable
centered
content
fulfilled
relaxed
relieved
satisfied
trusting

www.LoveCoachAcademy.com • info@LoveCoachAcademy.com • 707-295-7406

# INTIMATE INSIGHTS TO REVOLUTIONIZING INTIMACY

A Pocketful of Intimate Insights

This 4×6 pocketbook of quotes is an invitation to open your heart to a profound state of relating, free your mind of the emotional burdens, and awaken your senses to life.

**To order visit:** www.tziporahintimacy.com/books/

## The Intimate Truth Within Your Breath – A Simple Daily Practice to Clear Away Emotional Clutter and Live From Your Personal Tuned In, Turned On Power

Welcome to the Intimate Truth of Your Breath Home Practice with Tziporah!

Are you struggling with the stress of an over-busy mind and the "make it happen" mentality whether in home or professional relationships?

Are you feeling this stress is affecting the quality of your relationships? Is it stopping the flow of your own creativity or harming the way you communicate with your colleagues?

Do you desire more tuned in, turned on, spiritually alive connection's in your life?

The purpose of this audio series is to be a daily home practice to guide you through these stress-ors. You will begin to feel more connected with your own body, aware of your emotional needs, and feel more aligned with your personal power!

**To order visit:** www.tziporahintimacy.com/cds/

## Speaking Engagements

I am available to speak nationally and internationally.

With my mission to serve others and transform lives, I am available for media interviews, and en-lightening speaking engagements such as live events, tele classes, podcasts, and webinars. My work is uniquely powerful, life changing, and experiential-based. I bring a skillful and soulful style of dynamic feminine speaking and presence, that connects to any audience, especially women!

**To book me for an interview or speaking engagement, email: tziporah@tziporahintimacy.com.**

**Visit my media page to learn more:**
www.tziporahintimacy.com/tziporah-in-the-media/

## Private Mentoring for Individuals and Couples

Through personal mentoring, I lead individuals and couples to:

- Create and deepen your personal relationships
- Show up with a fierceness to share your truth and your gifts
- Develop a deep sense of presence and connection to spirit, so you are able to guide your cli-ents to have bigger breakthroughs
- Overcome your anxiety and inspire more action
- Revamp your love life and intimate relationships with reborn confidence
- Become more charismatic in any situation by leading from your heart and spirit!

**To learn more:**

www.tziporahintimacy.com/work-mentoring/